ENERGY

For Aslan,
and in memory of Regine

ENERGY
MEDICINE

Understanding energetic complementary therapies and how to make them work for you

John Hamwee

Vermilion
LONDON

1 3 5 7 9 10 8 6 4 2

First published in the United Kingdom in 2002 by Vermilion,
an imprint of Ebury Press, Random House,
20 Vauxhall Bridge Road, London SW1V 2SA

Random House Australia (Pty) Limited
20 Alfred Street, Milsons Point, Sydney,
New South Wales 2061, Australia

Random House New Zealand Limited
18 Poland Road, Glenfield, Auckland 10, New Zealand

Random House South Africa (Pty) Limited
Endulini, 5A Jubilee Road, Parktown 2193, South Africa

Random House UK Limited Reg. No. 954009
www.randomhouse.co.uk
A CIP catalogue record for this book
is available from the British Library

ISBN 0-0918 8224 9

Printed and bound by Mackays of Chatham plc, Chatham, Kent

Contents

Thanks

Dr Fritz Smith taught me practically everything I know about energy, and Meriel Darby practically everything I know about being a practitioner of energy medicine. From Ram Dass I learned to see the body and its illnesses in a new light.

Cathy Fischgrund is the best literary agent any author could wish for: without her belief in this book, at a time when I wasn't so sure, it would never have been written. This is the second time I have had the privilege of Judith Warren's editing, and her challenging questions and comments have forced me to think more clearly and hence write more clearly. Discussing the content of the book with Myra Connell helped enormously, as did her perceptive comments on early drafts. Felicity Candogan did the most scrupulous job of pointing out errors, inconsistencies and clumsy writing. In a few minutes Kate Carne solved a problem I'd been struggling with for months. At a time when I was flagging in the writing of it Kathryn Cave helped me to keep going. Nicholas Ellis, Scilla Elworthy and Hugh Miall read early drafts with great care and kindness, and made all kinds of helpful suggestions.

A time of change

Something very curious is happening in the world of medicine. On the one hand, the medical profession is held in high esteem, and, especially when faced with serious illness, patients show tremendous faith in their doctors. Practically everyone can remember a time when modern drugs and skilled medical care have helped them recover from illness or disease, and most people know someone who owes their life to them. Partly because of this and partly because technological sophistication is providing more and more treatments for more and more conditions, vast and ever-increasing resources are being poured into medical services. And however much is spent, it is never enough. In every country, whatever the particular system of funding, the public wants more to be spent on medicine – more than can be afforded.

On the other hand, the number of people who go to practitioners of alternative or complementary medicine is increasing exponentially. A small village in Gloucestershire has no less than four acupuncturists working in a clinic converted from the dairy of an old farmhouse. I often think of the farmer's wife, making butter and cheese there, and what she would have made of it. I wonder too at the speed of change; it would have been unimaginable even thirty years ago. All the people who go to that clinic, and to thousands of other clinics throughout the country, are choosing to take their complaints and their ailments to someone without a conventional medical training, and are seeking help from a system of medicine which, according to the vast majority of their doctors, doesn't work. In America, in 1999, more people went to a practitioner of complementary medicine than saw a doctor. Most of these patients are doing so not because of some ideological bias, but because conventional medicine hasn't made them better.

It's almost as if the public has a split personality. At the same time as it insists on more resources for conventional medicine, it is also choosing to use complementary medicine. What on earth is going on?

A large part of the answer stems from the dramatic success of conventional medicine. Penicillin is wonderful stuff; it works like magic. People who would have died of an infection seventy years ago are now up and about within a week. Cataract surgery restores sight with a ten minute operation. No-one would want to turn the clock back, to do without these and countless other practices which have become routine. But these successes have had a side effect. They have engendered a set of assumptions which are both wrong and dangerous.

One of these assumptions is that if there is no medical explanation for a patient's illness, then he or she isn't really ill. Many people have been to their doctor feeling unwell, and the doctor has undertaken a range of tests. The test results come back and they are all normal, so the patient is told either that there is nothing wrong or that their illness is probably psychosomatic, which means, in effect, 'you're imagining it'. These responses are commonplace, and they don't wash. Any such tests only look for certain things – usually deviations from some chemical norm. But what if the patient's illness has nothing to do with chemical norms, or if the norms don't apply in his or her particular case? That just means that the tests haven't, and can't, identify a cause. They don't show, far less prove, that the patient isn't ill. And even if the patient is 'imagining it' that doesn't make it any the less real, or any the less necessary to find some way of helping. Many of the people who try complementary medicine are those who have been given this kind of brush-off. They know they are unwell, and they are not willing to give up on getting better.

Another assumption is that if a particular treatment has a scientific basis then it must work. Take the case of a middle-aged woman who regularly had bad migraines, but was otherwise well and healthy. She went to her doctor, who carried out a thorough examination. He could find nothing wrong with her, except that she had high blood pressure. That seemed a sufficient explanation for the headaches. One effect of the high blood pressure will be to dilate blood vessels surrounding the brain, and that might well hurt. So he prescribed a beta- blocker, a drug which slows down the heart rate and reduces the force with which the heart contracts in order to pump blood round the system. As a result, her blood pressure came down, but unfortunately, her migraines didn't go away. The temptation, on the doctor's part, is to add another drug – the beta-blockers are working all right, so there must be something else going on too. Perhaps there is some infection of the meninges – the membranes that cover the brain – so he prescribes antibiotics, and so on, with the genuine risk that the drugs will have unpredictable and unwelcome side effects. The temptation on the patient's part is to feel obscurely guilty, a nuisance, to feel that she ought to be better so it is somehow her fault if she isn't.

And finally, there is an assumption that if a particular treatment doesn't have a scientific basis then it can't work. This is very common and very odd. Homeopathy is a great example. A homeopathic remedy is made, basically, by taking a natural substance and diluting it many many times. In fact, it is so diluted that usually there is not a single molecule of that substance left in the resulting remedy. Speaking chemically, therefore, whatever the healing property of the original substance, the remedy cannot work. There was an extensive review of clinical trials of homeopathy published in the *British Medical Journal* in 1991. The researchers concluded, 'Based on this evidence we would be ready to accept that homeopathy can be efficacious, if only the mechanism of action were more plausible … ' In other words, it works but because we don't understand how it works, it doesn't. Lewis Carroll would have been proud of them.

The truth is that the methods of science cannot account for the success of homeopathy, or of any of the other forms of energy medicine for that matter. And what that tells us is that the methods of science haven't yet been able to give a full account of how the body works. The researchers should have been delighted; they could have taken this as a spur and a challenge to improve the methods of science – there is a great tradition of scientists who have done just this when faced with some puzzle of nature. Instead they, and many others like them, buried their heads in the sand and fell back on the old assumption that if it can't be scientifically verified then it isn't true.

All this says, quite simply, is that as well as being remarkably successful in many ways, there are real limits to conventional medicine. There are some things it does brilliantly, and some things it can't reach at all. The apparently contradictory public attitude – wanting more resources for conventional medicine and going, in ever increasing numbers, to complementary practitioners – reflects a perfectly sensible appreciation of this fact. They want to have a hernia operation within a reasonable time, and they want to go to an osteopath or chiropractor if they have a bad back. They want a doctor to come to the house if someone is suddenly taken seriously ill, and they want to go to a homeopath or an acupuncturist if they are suffering from a chronic illness or just not feeling right.

The medical profession, with its suspicion of other forms and systems of medicine, and the politicians who are only concerned with the National Health Service, are lagging far behind the public wisdom. There isn't only one form of medicine, far less one form that can cure all.

Conventional medicine has a particular view of the human body, a particular perspective of illness and disease, a particular method of diagnosis, and particular forms of treatment. Energy medicine differs from conventional medicine in all these particulars – the rest of this book explains how and why – and therefore it works differently and will get different results. It is no criticism of either form of medicine to say that it cannot apply to every complaint of every patient. After all, a human being is a quite breathtakingly complex thing. Structurally, it is extraordinary. Just reach in every direction you can with your hand, and then try to imagine how the bones and tendons and muscles must be organized and stimulated to enable such an amazing variety of movements. Chemically it is astonishing – it transforms what you eat in a normal day into hair, fingernails, hormones, blood, semen, all distributed to the right places at the right times. The range and power of emotions that it feels, and the effects they have on all the other workings of the body are known to everyone, but hardly understood at all. Then there is the mystery of consciousness, and the even greater mystery of conscience and an awareness of the divine. And all these interact. We know that we're more likely to be ill when we're miserable, and that complaints tend to disappear when we fall in love. We all know too of people who have a severe illness or disability but who radiate joy to all those lucky enough to be in their presence. It is surely bizarre to believe that one perspective on this complexity could explain all, apply to all: surely wiser to try to find out what each perspective can reveal about some part of this whole, and what each suggests in the way of treatment.

As you will know if you've ever looked at a leaflet in a health food shop or complementary health clinic, there is a bewildering range of complementary therapies on offer. There are separate books on most of them and there are encyclopaedias which describe them briefly and seek to explain which one is good for which ailments. These books and leaflets emphasize the differences between the different therapies. It is true that each uses a different technique or set of techniques; true too that there isn't much overlap in the training of the different practitioners. But it is also true that they all have a lot in common, and there is a lot to be said for looking at the commonality. In one way or another, they all work deliberately and explicitly with energy – I will explain what this means in the next chapter – and the energy they all work with is the same, whatever the particular methods they use. It is a bit of an exaggeration to see all these therapies as the same, but it is less of an exaggeration, I think, than to see them all as different. Accordingly, it seems to me that it is helpful to look at them as simply examples of one system of medicine. Helpful if you are already having some sort of complementary therapy and want to understand what is going on in a treatment, and helpful if you want to have some confidence in the whole idea before you embark on any particular kind of treatment. The appendix lists the various therapies which I think of as techniques of energy medicine.

I also hope this book will be helpful to people who practise conventional medicine. More and more of their patients are also having some sort of energy medicine, and it is reasonable to suppose that, concerned with their patients' well-being, they want to know something about what this other system can offer and, just as important, what it cannot. They may also want to be able to discuss with their patients any reactions and responses to energy treatments: to be unable to do so would be to miss an important aspect of a patient's medical history. And for some of them it may begin to shed light on phenomena which can't be explained by their medical knowledge. A practising doctor wrote the following account:

> A man in his seventies had … a condition in his right hand which prevented him from fully closing it into a fist. He had been having this problem for more than ten years, during which time he had been thoroughly examined by a number of physicians and at various medical centers. No treatment had been helpful.
>
> I did not see his acupuncture treatment itself, but was present as he walked out of the consultation room,

*closing his hand fully for the first time in ten years.
He was ecstatic ... I learned that only a single needle
had been used and this had been placed in the soft
tissue of the opposite leg. The needle was kept in place
for about ten seconds, during which time the patient
was unaware of any pain. As I listened to this
treatment report my mind seemed to explode: none of
my medical experience could account for what I was
hearing ...*

*The struggle to resolve the apparent conflicts between
my own scientific training and the teachings of the
Eastern medical and energy models has been both
challenging and creative. And I believe that my
experience in this is not an uncommon one for many
physicians and health practitioners raised and trained
in the Western traditions. It is important to see that
out of this struggle a new understanding of the human
body is emerging along with a more complete model of
health and healing.*

Fritz Frederick Smith

This book doesn't try to prove that energy medicine works,
either by referring to current research or by explaining how it
can be validated scientifically; there are other books which do
that. I'm going to assume it works, at least much of the time
for most people, which is about as good as can be expected. But
the reason I don't go into whether or not it works is that I've
got other fish to fry. What I find fascinating and instructive in
all sorts of ways, ways which have very wide-reaching implications for anyone who has been ill and struggled to get better,
ways which have enormous implications for those trying to
provide health care, is how it works. After all, it does seem
strange. Sticking needles into people, giving them water which

has been shaken many times, using sounds or colours or aromas, pressing parts of the foot – how can any of these possibly bring people back to health?

By the end of this book the answer to that question will seem quite simple – things always seem quite simple when you understand them. Getting to that understanding doesn't require much technical knowledge; what it does require is a particular perception of the human body. What is it really like, this body we know so well in some ways and so little in others? What is really happening when it behaves in strange and painful ways, and what really helps it to heal?

Chapter 1

Images of the body

The body operates on energy, with energy, by energy: creating its own energy and taking in outside energy. A body is an individual energy machine. As you add together the parts of the machine appropriately or inappropriately, you get addition or you get subtraction from the energy of the machine as a whole. If you have a liver structure that is functioning very badly and the rest of your body is doing reasonably well, you will be taking away energy from the general store to keep the liver going. And the answer is, you won't feel so well. Because what you are registering when you say 'I feel' is the sum total of your energy.

Ida Rolf

I know it seems an odd question, but what is your body *like*? Is it like a machine, a tree, a horse – or like all of them in different ways? You probably didn't think that it might be like a movement, a river or a wind, though that is just as plausible an answer as a machine or a tree, because it is changing all the time as cells die and are replaced in a continuous flow. Your body, rather like a fountain, is constantly being created and recreated in more or less the same shape. This is not a particularly new idea.

> As the column of blue smoke from a cottage chimney in the breathless Summer Noon, or the steadfast seeming Cloud on the edge-point of a Hill in the driving air current, which momentarily condensed and recomposed, is the common phantom of a thousand successors; – such is the flesh, which our bodily eyes transmit to us; which our palates taste; which our hands touch.
>
> Samuel Taylor Coleridge

The analogy of a fountain, or smoke, or a cloud, is helpful in one particular way; it opens our eyes to the possibility that the body may change quickly. If a pebble gets stuck in the nozzle of a fountain the plume of water will change shape – remove the pebble and it changes back again. Here is an example of how this perception can form the basis of treatment:

A young woman had been feeling out of sorts, peculiar, not herself, for about a month. She couldn't say exactly when it started; with that kind of vague discomfort it's always difficult to know. In the course of the treatment I felt a difference between the two sides of her body. The right felt normal; bone and muscle yielded under my fingers and they responded as I worked. The left, by contrast, felt hard and brittle – strangely like glass. It seemed to have shrunk inwards into a tight and unresponsive mass. By the end of the treatment it felt a lot better, and a lot more like the right-hand side, so I hoped that she would start to feel better too.

After the treatment she asked me what I had noticed. Normally I keep my impressions to myself. They might well be mistaken or irrelevant and, more important, they might not help people to get well. But in this case, she and I had known each other for many years and there was a good deal of love and trust between us, so I told her. She mused on it, wondering how this contraction on one side of her body might have occurred. I asked her if she had had any sudden shock in the recent past. Then she remembered. She had been out a couple of times with a man, but had gradually felt more and more uneasy in his company and finally she told him she didn't want to see him any more. She was glad that he didn't know where she lived. About a week later there was a ring at her doorbell, late at night. She opened the door rather tentatively, and there he was on her doorstep. He was angry and abusive. She stood there listening, with the door half open, until she collected herself and shut the door. What she now realized is that when she opened the front door, the right-hand side of her body was behind it, but the left-hand side was exposed to the shock of his sudden appearance and to his anger.

To both of us that seemed to account for what I had noticed, and the imbalance between her left and right sides seemed a sufficient explanation for the way she had been feeling since. In any event, she got better after the treatment. It seems a simple enough story, but it raises many of the issues which will be discussed and developed in this book. Was what I was feeling real? How can treatment be applied to something so apparently nebulous? In what way does rectifying an imbalance, in this case between two sides of the body, clear up symptoms and help people to feel better?

Although this young woman never got to the stage of going to a doctor and having tests to find out what the matter was, plenty of people do so in similar circumstances. Sometimes the tests reveal nothing and the patients are told there is nothing the matter with them. But it would be more accurate to say that there is no deviation from some chemical or structural norm in the body; these are the things that Western medical tests can investigate. So if the problem stems from some other kind of disturbance or disruption – as in this case – then the tests won't unearth it. Or, for reasons which will become clear, they will only unearth it much later.

Many people report strange symptoms for which there is no known cause or cure; here are a few examples just from my own practice. An elderly woman gets a crop of bright red pinprick spots on her skin every day – though, for no apparent reason, they are worse on Friday. These spots fade into large dull red blotches as they clear, only to be replaced by a fresh crop the next day. A young man loses all his body hair over the course of a few weeks, except for a tuft of hair right on the top of his head. A middle-aged woman cannot touch anything red without breaking into a drenching sweat. I also treat people with all sorts of common conditions, like back pain, breathing difficulties, incontinence, frozen shoulders, arthritis, hair loss, migraines, irritable bowel syndrome, eczema. What all these people have in common is that the drugs they have been prescribed haven't made them better.

In treating them with energy medicine I don't just use a different set of techniques, I use a different system of thought. Energy medicine has its own diagnoses, its own classifications and categorizations: which is to say, its own way of looking at a person and his or her illness. It doesn't work to use the diagnosis from one system as a basis for the treatment techniques of another.

Mrs Levy is flushed with gratitude. 'The remedy you gave me for my asthma helped so much! Can I have some for my son? He has asthma, too.' I explain that the remedy isn't really for asthma – it's for her. Until people get the hang of the homeopathic perspective, they are often perplexed. 'You mean there isn't a homeopathic remedy for asthma?' As a matter of fact there are a hundred remedies listed in the standard repertories which have wheezing or asthmatic breathing in their provings. Which one we give depends on what other symptoms are present. Then we select a remedy that corresponds to that total picture. To use the homeopathic method properly we have to know more than one symptom. Are there also headaches? Pain in the legs? Even the asthma should be further characterized – what makes it better, what makes it worse. Is it aggravated by changes in seasons, is it prompted by humid weather? Do gastrointestinal upsets bring it on?

Dr Rudolph Ballentine

In the case of the young woman described at the start of this chapter, my diagnosis of a contracted left-hand side of her body would be useless to a Western doctor; he or she simply wouldn't have any treatment which could relate to that diagnosis. Similarly, the diagnosis of asthma is not much help to the homeopath quoted above.

Any Western reader will have been educated and brought up in the culture which has produced Western medicine, and will tend to take for granted its perception of the body, and therefore the way it characterizes illness and disease. The start of any understanding of energy medicine is to realize that there are other ways of perceiving the body.

Things and patterns

What we tend to notice are things: material objects. In medicine, this results in a search for the thing – the gene, the bacteria, the virus, the trapped nerve, the slipped disc – that has caused a disability or disease. A drug is then devised and prescribed to deal with the thing which is causing the problem, or surgery removes it.

The perception that the world is composed of things is built into the structure of our language. It is perplexing to ask what happens to your fist when you open your hand, or where your lap goes when you stand up. The reason these questions are perplexing is that, in our language, 'fist' and 'lap' are nouns; we think of them as things. But they aren't things at all. They are actions. They are what happens when you make a particular kind of movement. If we used verbs instead of nouns, there would be nothing perplexing. We wouldn't dream of wondering what happened to our walking when we come to a standstill. Similarly, we say 'it is raining', as if the 'it' was a thing, when there is really no 'it' at all. Absurd though it sounds, it would be more accurate to say something like 'raining is happening'.

To take a rather different example, everyone learns at school that a magnet has a north pole at one end and a south pole at the other. We are taught that these two poles are different – indeed 'polar opposites'. One attracts and the other repels. So if you put a magnet into a tray of iron filings, you'll see that some are pulled into the magnet at one pole and others pushed away from the opposite pole (Figure 1a). But there is another way of perceiving this phenomenon. It's easiest to see if you cut the magnet in half. Then you notice that the attraction and repulsion look like parts of one flow through and beyond the metal (Figure 1b). However many times you cut the magnet, you see the same pattern (Figure 1c). It makes just as much sense to classify the north and south poles as

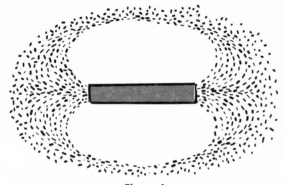

Figure 1a

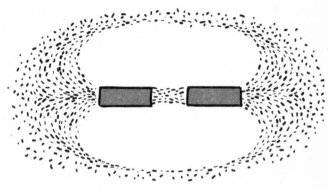

Figure 1b

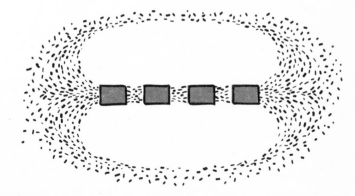

Figure 1c

stages of one continuous and coherent flow as it does to see them as opposite things.

Noticing the flow through a magnet, or saying that 'raining is happening' is much closer to the Eastern perception of the world. Generalizing, what is noticed is not so much the thing, but the process, the movement, the change. Probably the oldest book in any civilization is the *I Ching*, or *Book of Changes*. And the key concept that describes and explains the processes of change is what is known as 'qi' in China and 'prana' in India. It used to be translated as 'life-force' but is now more usually called energy. In fact, there is no adequate translation of these words because we do not have an exact equivalent concept in the West; and the reason we do not have an equivalent concept is because we don't normally see the world in that way. Perceiving things, we are blind to processes.

At this point I first wrote 'What makes things change is an absorbing question in the East...', then I realized that even in formulating that sentence I was myself thinking about this in a Western way. 'What makes things change...' suggests that there is some thing which is doing it. A better attempt at the question which much Eastern philosophy and medicine addresses would be 'What are the patterns, the rhythms, the dynamics of change?'

The obvious starting point in investigating the patterns of change is to observe the rhythms and dynamics of the natural world. There is contrast between day and night, winter and summer, the in-breath and the out-breath, each of which changes inexorably into the other. This, I imagine, is the source of the Chinese classification of all aspects of the world, including energy, into yin and yang. Winter, the night-time and the out-breath are classified as yin; that is, they are passive and quiet. Or, to make the same point more precisely, yin energy has these qualities. Summer, the daytime and the in-breath, by contrast, are yang; their energy has an active, dynamic, forceful quality. One is not better and the other

Figure 2

worse; both kinds of energy are essential parts of the whole. It is the same whatever whole you take – whether it is a cell of the body, which has both what we call a negative and a positive electrical charge, a magnet with its two poles, a human being who needs periods of activity and periods of rest, or the world itself with its seasons. Although yin and yang appear so different, they are the two sides of the same coin, the two halves of the one full year, full day or full breath. This is wonderfully represented in the famous symbolic representation of yin and yang (Figure 2).

The symbol elaborates the basic idea. The area of yin, which is black, and the area of yang, which is white, are equal. In other words, the whole is seen as being made up of these two opposites in balance. That's an ideal; what works best. It may be that in life they aren't in balance. For a person with asthma, it may be harder to breathe in than to breathe out, or it may be that one year the winter is much longer than usual and the summer much shorter; but these are seen as deviations from the norm, which is balance. Also, you will see that the area of yin has in it a small amount of yang – the white dot; similarly, the area of yang has within it an area of yin – the black dot. That's because all this is relative. Nothing is absolutely yin or absolutely yang. Night-time has the potential of daytime within it, summer the potential of winter, and vice versa. The Chinese always talk of things being 'predominantly yin' or 'predominantly yang' to make sure they don't overlook this inherent capacity for change.

Any change can be seen as a change in the amount or quality of yin in relation to yang. At dusk, the strength of yang energy fades and the strength of yin energy starts to take over; the same thing happens to a person when he or she goes to bed. The reverse happens at dawn and when a person gets up in the morning. It might seem as if this is merely playing with words; why bother to describe what happens in this way? A full answer to that question will take the whole book; the short answer is that this idea, this classification of aspects of change, makes possible both sophisticated diagnoses of people who are unwell, and highly specific treatments for their ailments.

Observing the seasons is another traditional route to understanding change. Spring is the time of growth, youth, newness. Shoots push up through the earth, buds break into blossom, birds mate and lay eggs, there is clear bright sunshine and strong winds. It is characterized by dynamic activity. By contrast, the energy of autumn is one of contraction; leaves fall, plants die back and many animals start their hibernation; the air is often still. And each season changes into the next in a never-ending cycle.

These fundamental movements from day to night and from season to season are directly relevant to medicine. There is no reason to believe that the nature of movement and change will be different in us humans; in fact, there is good reason to believe it will be much the same because we are part of the natural world. The basic life cycle of animals and trees is the same as ours. Nor is it far-fetched to see one full sequence of the seasons as analogous to the full sequence of a life, with birth in the spring and death in the depths of winter. In short, the Eastern view goes like this; there is a natural process, an orderly pattern of change in progress, which governs human beings as it governs everything else. The macrocosm and the microcosm are subject to the same laws. This view is often summarized by the aphorism, 'as above, so below'. That is, if you find a pattern in the largest processes of nature you will find it in the smallest ones too. Fascinatingly, the recent discoveries of fractal mathematics leads to the same view.

Energy medicine is based on observation of the rhythms and patterns of change in the natural world, on recognition of versions of these patterns in the human body, and on the formulation of some key concepts with which to organize the knowledge gained. Knowing the general behaviour of energy in the body, means that change towards illness can be identified in particular individuals and treatments formulated to turn it round into change towards health.

Energy

We all notice energy in ourselves and others. Some days we feel dispirited, we drag ourselves from one task to the next and say we have no energy. At other times we feel like working all day and partying all night and say we've got bags of it. We are sensitive to other people's energy too. We pick up when a person is feeling flat or getting weary, and we are lifted by being with someone in high spirits and with a zest for life. When a work group feels that it has been asked to meet impossible goals or accomplish an impossible task, its energy and productivity levels go down. Although there are many sophisticated methods of diagnosing the state of a person's energy, they all amount to refinements of this basic act of noticing.

One refinement I have already mentioned is to notice the relative strengths of a person's yin and yang energy. A man comes for treatment complaining of red weals which erupt on his skin, especially on his palms and lower arms. He is a person who never stops, holding down a stressful job and going out every evening. He loves being the boss at work, and being the life and soul of the party, endlessly joking with everyone he meets. Even on holiday abroad, he doesn't rest, but is up and about all through the middle of the day, even when everyone else, including the locals, is taking a siesta. He says that he doesn't notice the heat, and anyway he always has trouble sleeping, even at night. All these signs and symptoms point to the same conclusion – that he has an excess of yang energy. The weals come from heat in his system and heat is a manifestation of yang energy, as is his insomnia, relentless joking and ceaseless activity.

By contrast, imagine someone who is withdrawn and taciturn, gets up late in the day, looks pale, and suffers from regular bouts of bronchitis. He has not recovered from the ending of a relationship some years before, and broods on his grief. Yin energy predominates in him. You might say that his energy is like that of autumn; a time when nature seems to contract as the abundance of summer is lost. Linking autumn and loss, the inner experience and the outer season, is not just an Eastern idea; Shakespeare expresses it in one of his sonnets:

That time of year thou mayest in me behold

When yellow leaves, or none, or few do hang

Upon those boughs which shake against
   the cold,

Bare ruin'd choirs where late the sweet birds sang.

These examples suggest that a person's emotional state, as well as his physical illness and even his appearance are all consistent. They are all aspects of something – it isn't quite personality or disposition. In fact there isn't really a good word for it in English. In the East, of course, they would all be seen as aspects of a person's energy.

The idea that the state and nature of a person's energy will express itself in consistent ways, both physically and emotionally, means that the diagnosis of what is troubling a patient will not, cannot, separate the mind and the body. Both will be pointing in the same direction; both will provide clues as to the energy state which lies behind the signs and symptoms of distress. Until a practitioner is sure that her assessment of that energy state can account for both mental and physical symptoms, she has not arrived at a plausible diagnosis.

Most of us have a rather vague idea that the mind is in the brain which is in the head, and that it rules over the whole body. I suppose it comes, in part, from normal experiences like deciding to change channel on the TV, reaching for the remote control, and pressing the right button. The arm and finger are obeying the command, implementing the decision which comes from the head. It is as if the body were a large organization with the boss's office on the top floor and the minions below scurrying about to carry out orders. But there is plenty of evidence that what we consider the functions of the mind – thinking and memory – are not solely in the brain.

I felt weak, had an almost constant headache, and sweated so heavily at night that the bed was soaked in the morning. I often told my wife that there was some form of toxic energy in me that I could not describe, but when I told my doctors about this sense of impending doom that I seemed to be experiencing in my heart, they responded that their tests showed nothing they considered abnormal and that I was just under stress from my clinical work. My brain accepted their diagnosis, but my heart remained very worried.

> *As weeks went on, I became constantly nauseated,*
> *food repulsed me, and my every move was*
> *accompanied by severe pain ... I told my doctors that,*
> *despite their dismissal of my symptoms as being 'only*
> *in my head', it was my heart that kept telling me I*
> *was dying... After one particularly tearful discussion*
> *with my primary physician about a very sick feeling*
> *deep in my heart, he impatiently said, 'I give up. I'll*
> *do a CAT scan just to put your mind at rest. For*
> *God's sake, man, you're a scientist. Use your brain.*
> *Don't think with a pump.'*
>
> *During the CAT scan, the doctors and nurses behind*
> *the screen had their first glimpse of a soccer-ball-sized*
> *tumor ...*

Paul Pearsall

This scientist knew that there was something seriously amiss because his heart, not his head, kept telling him he was dying.

Another angle on this issue comes from other cultures which have believed for centuries that the organs don't only carry out physical functions but mental ones too. The Chinese, for example, have the term 'hsin hsin' which is usually translated as 'the thinking heart'. It's an odd, awkward phrase. That's because it is untranslatable, really; in this culture, we don't believe that the heart can think, so there is no word for the Chinese idea. But, in our language, there are remnants of a belief that the heart thinks – and thinks somewhat differently from the brain. We might say 'I can't find it in my heart to do this', which means that it makes sense to do it, but there is some other, more important, and probably inexpressible reason for not doing it. To take something 'to heart' means to take it more seriously than just a passing thought, idea, or piece of information. And of course, we learn things not 'off by head' but 'off by heart'.

To see the mind and body as linked in this way means that the notion of psychosomatic illness, which has rather crept in by the back door of conventional medicine and often been treated as something of an impostor, is centre stage here. Energy will manifest in thoughts and emotions as much as in symptoms and pain. It is not just unhelpful to say to a person that his or her illness is 'all in the mind', it is inaccurate too. Modern scientific research, such as that carried out by Candace Pert, makes it clear that intelligence is diffused throughout the body, and touch on a knee or a foot can bring back long-forgotten memories. Contrary to common belief, there is nothing self-indulgent or hysterical about a psychosomatic illness. A leading cancer surgeon, writes:

> *Years of experience have taught me that cancer and indeed nearly all diseases are psychosomatic. This may sound strange to people accustomed to thinking that psychosomatic ailments are not truly 'real', but believe me they are.*

> Bernie S. Siegel

Additionally, the diagnosis will also have to take into account the state of the person's spirit. Spirit is a rather vague word, and in the East there are much more precise words for the same idea. However, it is clear that by spirit we mean something different from, and somehow deeper than, thoughts or emotions. Being in good spirits isn't quite the same as being happy. It shows in people's eyes and in the way they walk, in the tone of voice and in attitudes to others; all of which are only mildly affected by temporary emotional states. It is contagious too; it is enlivening to be with people who are in good spirits and depressing to be with those whose spirits are low. The state of a person's spirit is often the most obvious clue to the state of their energy, and very commonly it is a depression of spirit that really brings people to seek help from a practitioner, even though they often think it necessary to present themselves as having some troublesome physical symptom.

To regard body, mind and spirit as inseparable will affect not only diagnosis but also treatment. Treating a person's energy will have consequences for all three. In the case of a man who has chronic lower back pain, for example, the treatment will probably seek to change the quality or quantity of his energy primarily at the physical level. That is, the focus of the treatment will be on the energy which supports the spine or the surrounding muscles. Still, that treatment will also have an effect on the mind and the spirit too, because treating energy is bound to affect all three levels. And it makes perfect sense to give a treatment which does so, because the pain itself will also have had an effect on his mind and spirit. He may be upset that he can no longer do the heavy lifting jobs which he once did for his wife, and that may have diminished his self-image as a capable and helpful husband. He may no longer be able to play some sport he loved. As a result he may have bouts of depression. Treating his energy should help with the depression as well as with the back pain. Of course, if his back heals after surgery or drugs, there may be the same result; relieved of pain, he may recover his self-regard and cheerfulness. But there is a big difference between seeing this as a benign side effect and seeing it as an integral part of the diagnosis and treatment.

More interestingly, it may be that his back pain is not the primary focus of treatment. It may be a symptom of a problem with his energy at the mental level. Suppose that this man is having great difficulty in coping with his job, has financial problems, is worried that he isn't giving enough time to the children, and feels unsupported in his marriage. He cannot stop work because of the financial pressure, nor does he believe there is anyone he can turn to for help. He worries constantly and feels he is carrying a huge burden of responsibility on his own. In these circumstances, it wouldn't be surprising if he cracked; if he became ill as a way, unconsciously, of making it all right for him to stop. Nor would it be surprising if the particular way in which he became ill were with chronic lower back pain. He can no longer support the burden he is carrying, and it is the lumbar spine which supports the weight of the whole of the upper body and head. In this case, treatment may well be directed mainly to the mental level, to the energy which normally enables him to think clearly and act decisively but which has been disorganized or disturbed by all the worry. If that is restored to normal, he will find it easier to cope, to sort out his financial situation, to get some help, and, in consequence, his back pain will probably clear up. Again, it may be that the same effect could be achieved by prescribing tranquillizers, perhaps with some counselling too; but that would be an unusual prescription for back pain. One of the strengths of energy medicine is that the same style of treatment can be directed to whichever level of the system seems to offer the best prospect for healing.

The energy body

The notion that what we regard as the separate aspects of a person, such as their physical health and their emotional state, are all consistent expressions of their energy suggests a different way of thinking about the body. Normally we perceive the body as a physical object, distinct from all other objects and from the space in which it lives. What are the implications of seeing it not only as an object but also as energy?

One implication is that this energy may have a shape or form which is not identical to that of the physical body. It might extend beyond the skin, so that the body lives in it rather as an astronaut lives in his space suit. In fact, there is quite a lot of evidence that this is true. It is a common experience that some people seem to take up a lot of space, even though they aren't particularly big. Perhaps their energy extends further beyond them than is normal. Another example is the uncomfortable feeling you suddenly get when being approached by someone you don't care for, that you don't want them to get any closer. Perhaps you are sensing the boundary between your energy and that of the other person, and you don't want yours to be invaded, so to speak. With someone you love, of course, the moment when you are close enough to feel somehow connected, overlapping, is a delight.

In addition, there are people who claim to be able to see auras around the human body; that is areas of colour or light which extend beyond the body and which are clearly differentiated from the surrounding space. Few people have bothered to try to find out if there is any validity in what they are seeing. One who has done so is Valerie Hunt, a distinguished neurophysiologist, who has been a professor at three American universities. She asked eight people who claimed to have this skill to give reports of the extent and nature of the auras of a group of subjects, and she found that all eight reports were remarkably consistent. It seemed that there was something there, beyond mere subjective impressions. In the spirit of a true inquirer, she then devised an experiment to measure the amount and the frequency of electromagnetic energy given off by each subject. Perhaps her instruments, normally used to test muscular activity, might pick up and measure whatever was being reported by the aura readers. When she put together the reports of the aura readers and the measurements from her equipment, she again found them to be consistent; that is her scientific test corroborated the perceptions of the aura readers.

She also tested the common experience I referred to earlier, of feeling contact with another person when they get close.

> ... we placed two blindfolded people back to back in chairs so that only their auric fields could touch.

Neither subject was consciously aware of the other.
Each was instrumented to record auric changes ...
With amazement we watched the interface and the
change of each field. Some people did not interact well
through their fields; in fact, sometimes two fields
would remain absolutely separate, retaining their
individual patterns. With others, one field totally
dominated the other, that is, one changed while the
other did not ... Sometimes both fields changed to
become identical, yet unlike either beginning field.

Valerie V. Hunt

This makes me think of people I know. With one, for example, after some time in her presence I end up feeling dominated although I can find nothing in the conversation we have had to explain my feeling. With another, I always feel lighter, 'fluffed up' after we have met, even though we may have hardly talked. And it is a familiar sensation to have spent time sitting next to and talking with someone, but to feel that there has been no real contact between us.

The results of this research are consistent both with our everyday experience and with the notion in Eastern medicine that a person's energy has its own dimensions and qualities. One way of summing this up is to say that human beings have an energy body as well as a physical body. That energy body is closely linked to the physical body and is roughly the same size, but it has its own shape, boundaries and nature.

Just as with the physical body, an energy body has both a general aspect, common to all human beings, and an idiosyncratic, individual aspect. If you were to look at the rib cages of a group of people, even people of the same age, these two aspects would be obvious. On the one hand, everyone has a rib cage, and it has the same number of bones arranged in the same way. On the other hand, you would also be struck by the remarkable diversity. In one person, the ribs are large and close together; in another, they are small and widely spaced. In one person, the rib cage is long, dropping steeply on either side from the centre of the chest; in another, it is short and the ribs curve sharply towards the back. And if you have experience in touching bone you would notice other differences too. One person's ribs would feel light and springy, another's dense and hard, yet another's brittle and fragile.

The same is true of the energy body. There are commonalities and regularities in the energy bodies of all human beings. There is a basic anatomy of energy – there's more about this in a later chapter. At the same time, each person's energy body is distinctive and unmistakable, rather like each person's fingerprint or DNA. A practitioner of energy medicine learns to identify the individual energy body of a patient, and to notice its unique qualities. This is good diagnostic information which will suggest a strategy for treatment.

There will usually be an overall quality. It may be scattered and chaotic, and the patient may find it hard to concentrate and stick to a task, in which case the practitioner will aim to introduce order and coherence in the energy body. It may be flat, dull and listless, leading to apathy and depression, and what is required is a stimulation and a revitalization. It may be strong in some areas, but weak in others; dense and compacted in one part but clear and lively elsewhere. There are endless variations – Figure 3 shows some visual representations of energy bodies. And, knowing the state of a patient's energy body when he or she is well, makes it easier to see when something is wrong, to pick up the signs of impending illness or disease. This is why energy medicine can work so well as preventive medicine.

The implications are profound. As I mentioned earlier, every doctor as well as every practitioner of complementary medicine, sees patients who have strange disorders or complaints. Here is a striking example.

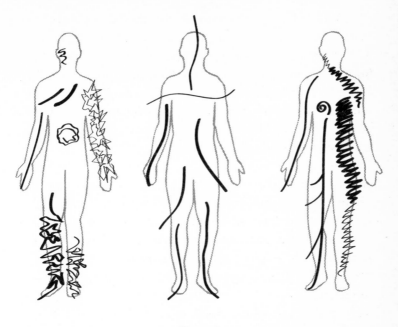

Figure 3

A thirty-year-old woman turns up at the Emergency Room of an American hospital saying that she is having a heart attack. The doctors carry out the usual tests but can find nothing wrong with her heart. She turns up the next week, saying the same, with the same outcome. After she has been over twenty times, they understandably start to lose patience with her; they suggest she has psychiatric help, which she refuses indignantly. Finally a new doctor joins the hospital, one who has also had training in energy medicine. Mainly to relieve her obvious level of stress, he suggests that he does an energy medicine treatment. In the course of diagnosis he discovers that the energy of her heart is very low, and that what little there is seems chaotic, disturbed. He gives her an appropriate treatment, at the end of which she says she feels very much better. As she is leaving the room she turns to him and says 'Do you think the treatment will help me to recover from a rape?'

Of course the rape affected her heart. She must have been heartbroken. She knew that it had been wounded, but the wound didn't show up as an injury to the tissue; it was, as yet, an injury to the energy body. What she was feeling would only be mysterious if the heart were regarded as merely a thing, a physical pump.

Returning to the more usual, it may be that those common complaints which do not respond well to conventional medicine are primarily the manifestations of disorder in the energy body. This is the conclusion which Valerie Hunt draws from her research:

> *Electromedical researchers believe that each disease or functional disturbance has its own energy field which must be reversed before healing can take place. Probably illness is a disturbance first in the energy field and healing is the restoration of that field to health. Soon we should be able to show unequivocally that field disturbance precedes all tissue changes. When tissue is diseased, the problem is already far advanced.*

Valerie V. Hunt

This, then, is the reason why I said at the start of the chapter it might be a long time before conventional medical tests on the young woman who opened her front door would reveal that anything was amiss. The problem has to be 'far advanced' before the tissue change is discernible.

All this is directly relevant to the most fundamental principle of medical practice, 'do no harm'. Any medical intervention will have an affect on the energy body as well as the physical body. But if the person making the intervention is unaware of the patient's energy body, then, with an intervention that is well intentioned and perfectly sensible in relation to the physical body, he or she may be damaging the energy body. If 'illness is a disturbance first in the energy field' then the consequence of any such intervention could be illness or dysfunction, sooner or later in the physical body. This is as much a caution to practitioners of energy medicine as it is to those of conventional medicine.

In the rest of this book I will take what I have set out in this chapter for granted. Namely, that energy flows through the human body, and forms a coherent whole which may be called the energy body. The way in which that energy flows in an individual, and its qualities, provides a partial but immensely useful explanation of a person's physical, mental and spiritual state. It also provides a way of understanding and explaining the nature of any change, which may be in the direction of disease or of health. And all this holds out the alluring prospect that a system of medicine which treats the energy body may be able to help heal those whose pain, illness or disabilities do not respond well to conventional medicine. There is the even more alluring prospect that it may help to prevent them.

Chapter 2

The meaning of illness

I met him for the first time in his home in Puerto Rico just a few weeks before his ninetieth birthday. I was fascinated by his daily routine ... His various infirmities made it difficult for him to dress himself. Judging from his difficulty in walking and from the way he held his arms, I guessed he was suffering from rheumatoid arthritis. His emphysema was evident in his laboured breathing. He came into the living room on Marta's arm. He was badly stooped. His head was pitched forward and he walked with a shuffle. His hands were swollen and his fingers were clenched.

Even before going to the breakfast table, Don Pablo went to the piano – which, I learned, was a daily ritual. He arranged himself with some difficulty on the piano

*bench, then with discernible effort raised
his swollen and clenched fingers above
the keyboard.*

*I was not prepared for the miracle that was
about to happen. The fingers slowly
unlocked and reached toward the keys like
the buds of a plant towards the sunlight.
His back straightened. He seemed to breathe
more freely. Now his fingers settled on the
keys. Then came the opening bars of Bach's
Wohltemperiere Klavier; played with great
sensitivity and control ... Then he plunged
into a Brahms concerto and his fingers,
now agile and powerful, raced across the
keyboard with dazzling speed. His entire
body seemed fused with the music; it was
no longer stiff and shrunken but supple
and graceful and completely free of its
arthritic coils.*

Norman Cousins

This inspiring story of the elderly Pablo Casals raises a fascinating question. The author who 'guessed he was suffering from rheumatoid arthritis' knew a good deal about medicine, so he was probably right. And yet, and yet … there were the fingers racing across the keyboard and there was his whole body supple and graceful. He was doing the impossible. How?

The basic answer to that question, which I want to elaborate in this chapter, is that illness may not be quite what we think it is. Some of our views about it are entirely personal, based on our particular experiences, but many of them are cultural, shared by most people in our society. Here are some common attitudes to illness:

It is something that happens to us. It's a bit like terrible weather, only worse; it comes from outside and unless we have abused our bodies grossly, falling ill is completely beyond our control. That's why we feel sorry for people who are ill; they have been unlucky.

It is an enemy. After all, it brings a lot of pain and discomfort, can stop us enjoying ourselves and earning a living, and can disrupt all our plans for the future. Like any enemy, therefore, it must be defeated.

It is caused by something specific. That's why there isn't a cure for cancer; no one has yet found the thing that causes it.

In going into battle against illness, we call on allies who know the enemy and have special weapons which they can deploy against it. In other words, we need the help of a doctor. We don't really believe we'll get better without that help.

> When our troublesome symptoms cease, the
> illness has gone and we are healthy again.

I'm sure you'll recognize at least some of these; after all, our health system is based on them. In fact, any system of medicine is based on a set of ideas, beliefs and assumptions about the nature of illness. You can't even diagnose what's wrong with someone unless you have some theory of what illness is – without such a theory what would you look for? What would you find significant? One theory entails taking a person's blood pressure and comparing it to a norm, another theory demands careful note of the colour and covering of particular areas of the tongue. Nor could you work out what would be an effective treatment. If you believe, for example, that a particular illness is caused by a virus, then you look for that virus in the body, and if you find it you prescribe a medicine to kill it. If you don't know about viruses you'll look for something else, and then devise a completely different treatment based on what you found. This may seem awfully obvious, but it is overlooked all the time. To make any sense of the practices of energy medicine, you first have to understand its view of illness.

Balance

Human beings stand and walk rather precariously on two narrow feet and two long legs. If you look at someone standing normally, you'll appreciate the difficulty. Our upper bodies, especially the shoulders, are too wide and too far from the ground for us to be really stable; animals which walk on four legs, except giraffes I suppose, have an easier time of it. We manage, in large part, because all our muscles are paired. For each muscle that stretches a part of the body (they are called 'extensors') there is one which contracts it (called 'flexors'). These muscles constantly balance each other.

If they don't, maybe one of the extensors of the back has been damaged, then the physical consequences can be severe. It will be hard to walk or even to stand upright. Mental states can upset physical balance too. When a person is depressed, for example, the flexors will be more activated than the extensors; typically you will notice that the back slumps and the body curls inwards. If the depression goes on for a long time, this gets to be a vicious circle. Spending a long time curled up, the flexor muscles become chronically shortened; so to do normal things like walking and making tea requires the extensor muscles to work very hard. This takes a lot of energy, and as a result the person feels tired all the time and can't face going out and having fun – which is depressing. Helping the flexor muscles to stretch out again is a perfectly sensible treatment for depression; restoring physical balance will go a long way to restoring mental balance too.

This is a simple example of a fundamental notion in energy medicine. It is a bit of an exaggeration, but not much, to say that all illness is seen as a lack of balance.

Before I go on to explain this fully, I want to consider an obvious objection. What about germs? They cause illnesses, don't they? What has balance got to do with it? Well, there is no doubt at all that some germs are highly infectious. If you are living in an area where there is a cholera outbreak and you contract the disease, there isn't much point in looking more deeply into the cause of your illness. But few germs are so virulent and few situations so dramatic. Much more often it isn't at all clear that germs are the cause of disease, although they are practically always present in diseased tissue.

I suspect that we will eventually come round to the idea that most diseases involve disorder on multiple levels, and that the proliferation of bacteria, fungi or viruses is merely one (physical) manifestation of a multi-level, complex disturbance. If that is true, then

virtually every disease will be found to have a typical
psychological picture, a distinctive energetic
derangement, a well-defined metabolic or biochemical
expression, and a characteristic microbe that tends to
grow. Which of these levels is playing the more
'causal' role might vary from case to case – or even
from moment to moment in the same case.

Dr Rudolph Ballentine

Just as the discovery of germs in the nineteenth century led doctors to think that they were a sufficient explanation for many illnesses, so now, as more and more is being discovered about our genetic make-up, more and more illnesses are being attributed to genes. A few precise and well-established causal connections have been established: a mutated version of a gene in chromosome 4 leads inexorably, sooner or later, to an illness called Huntington's Chorea. But this is unusual. Normally it isn't correct to say that specific genes cause specific illnesses. Although vastly more is known about genes than was ever thought possible in 1953 when the structure of DNA was first mapped, we are still a long way from knowing the exact connection between the vast majority of illnesses and a particular genetic pattern, and even further from a full understanding of the interaction between genes and diet, genes and pollution, genes and stress and so on.

The brain, the body and the genome are locked, all
three, in a dance. The genome is as much under the
control of the other two as they are controlled by it.
That is partly why genetic determinism is such a
myth. The switching on and off of human genes can
be influenced by conscious or unconscious external
action … We instinctively assume that bodily
biochemistry is cause whereas behaviour is effect,

an assumption we have taken to a ridiculous extent by
considering the impact of genes on our lives … Far
from us lying at the mercy of our omnipotent genes, it
is often the genes that lie at the mercy of us. If you go
bungee jumping or take a stressful job, or repeatedly
imagine a terrible fear, you will raise your cortisol
levels, and the cortisol will dash about the body
switching on genes.

Matt Ridley

In other words, take the question about causes of illness one stage back. Granted that there are germs, and that they can cause havoc, the question is 'why did they get a hold here, in this person, at this time, and why didn't the body's own self-healing processes – which are so effective practically all the time – deal with them?' Or, to apply the same kind of question to illnesses thought to be caused by genes, it is sensible to ask under what circumstances or conditions does a particular genetic pattern spring into action and start to disrupt the normal functioning of the body. The general answer which energy medicine gives to these questions is that an unbalanced system is vulnerable, weakened, and unable to heal itself. That gives germs the opportunity to flourish. They are one symptom, there will be others too, of a lack of balance. Hence the route back to full health is to restore balance.

One of the striking achievements of energy medicine is to take this general notion of balance and to pinpoint how it operates in the body. It is all well and good as a kind of common sense, like 'moderation in all things', as a kind of philosophical ideal, like 'the golden mean', or as an analogy from nature, for example that with too much rain and not enough sun the potatoes go mouldy. But it takes a giant leap of the imagination and intellect to show precisely how it can cause oedema, tendonitis or Crohn's disease. Although it will take most of the book to explain that fully, for the moment I want to distinguish two kinds of imbalance, two levels of illness.

The first level is where the energy body, or a part of it, simply isn't getting the energy it needs in order to work properly. It's as simple and obvious as not getting enough water to drink – dehydration brings on painful symptoms quickly – or not getting enough vitamin C, which leads to scurvy. And indeed, to a practitioner, such a basic imbalance is usually just as easy to diagnose and to treat as dehydration or scurvy. Until it is treated there is no point in looking any deeper for the cause of illness. Although the basic imbalance may not be the whole story, and more precise treatment may be needed for a full recovery, nothing is going to do much good until that is put right. For example, for a couple of days before I wrote this I wasn't feeling right. My head was fuzzy and I couldn't think clearly; waves of weariness would sweep over me at odd times, and if I couldn't just give in to them and go to sleep, it was a real struggle to carry on. My legs felt sluggish and somehow blocked up inside; they were uncomfortable in bed at night and achy in the daytime. Coincidentally, a friend who is also an acupuncturist came for lunch today and I told her how I was feeling. By feeling my pulse in various positions on both hands (there's more about this in Chapter 4) she diagnosed the problem as a basic imbalance of this kind and gave me a treatment. With that one treatment all my symptoms cleared up immediately (and I could get back to writing this book). Although this is a simple example of a minor problem, restoring some basic imbalance can make all the difference to serious and chronic illnesses.

The second level is where the imbalance is more complex, and seems to be the outcome of a whole set of circumstances. It usually takes some time, and a number of treatments, to work out quite what the imbalance is like and quite how to help it change. The man with lower back pain in the last chapter is a good example. In his body there will certainly be unusual tension in some muscles and unusual slackness in others, some joints may have become tighter than they should be and others looser, nerves may have become compressed and so on. That's one manifestation of imbalance At the same time, the wilful effort to keep going will have had an effect on his mind as well as his body. A rather grim determination may have taken over and left no room for relaxation, or even joy, and he may well be irritable and take offence when his colleagues, trying to help him to take it easy, tease him about what a tartar he's become. That's another manifestation of imbalance. His energy body will have become distorted in all sorts of ways, and it may not be immediately obvious where to start with treatment. It's a bit like a ball of string which has become unwound in a drawer and is mixed up with lots of pens, paper clips, bluetack and rubber bands. You know you'll have to find one end of the string to sort out the mess, but you may have to root around for a while to find it.

There is one other big difference between this level of imbalance and the first one. At the first level, the treatment usually does the job, and the patient need do nothing. At the second level, the treatment will be vastly more effective if the patient is willing to collaborate in understanding the illness and what he or she needs to do to get better. Bundled up in that complex of circumstances will be, to a greater or lesser extent, some ways in which the patient is leading his or her life that aren't helping. They may be partial causes of the illness or they may be getting in the way of recovery. At the simplest level, someone with asthma needs to give up smoking, or someone with arthritis will have to cut out orange juice. It's more difficult when the patient really needs to make an emotional change, like accepting that a relationship is over or coming to terms with the infirmities of old age, or appreciating that not all those who disagree with him or her are enemies.

Quite often, at this level, the change the patient needs to make is critical. A man comes to see me with a painful knee. He loves playing golf, and is about to go on holiday with his partner who is a keen golfer too. A few days before, his left knee started to hurt badly; he didn't fall or do anything weird to it, it just came on. And now he's worried that he won't be able to enjoy his holiday. When I examine the knee there's no doubt that he has a physical problem; it's swollen and hot to the touch, and some of the muscle above it is in spasm. As I talk to him I realize how busy he must be. An active, dynamic man in his early forties, with a responsible job in a large organization, he also does a lot for his widowed father, and for his stepchildren, and he often goes out in the evenings too – but then he's been doing all that for years. Suddenly he starts to tell me about a job he's on at the moment. He's helping out a company which his organization has recently taken over, and which is in a terrible mess. He likes the people in that company a lot and they all depend on him to pull it round. He tells me that it is really more than he wants to do, but he can't leave them in the lurch. I ask him how it feels to have that responsibility. He replies immediately, 'they're leaning on me; everyone's leaning on me'. Then he adds, 'they're like a wall that's about to collapse. They are all permanently falling down and I'm permanently propping them up'. As he says it he blushes and his body posture changes (there's an explanation for these kinds of reactions in a later chapter). The atmosphere between us changes too: it becomes still and highly charged.

We talk a little about the situation he finds himself in, and the difficulties it is causing him. He understands perfectly that he can't go on propping them up indefinitely. After a while he goes quiet and looks down. Then he lifts his head and says, more to himself than to me, 'I'll find someone else to help the company, and I'll be out of there within two months.' He says it with an air of finality, as if it is a promise, a commitment.

Clearly, there's nothing more to talk about, so he gets onto the couch and I prepare to work on the knee. But when I put my hands on it, it isn't hot any more and the swelling is visibly reduced. He looks better too – he has more colour in his face, more vivacity somehow. I think about what to do. I check the muscles and the spasm has gone. I'm playing for time because of the wise old rule 'if it isn't broken, don't fix it'. I don't want to interrupt the change that is happening – above all I don't want to make his knee worse. Finally, I make up my mind not to treat it specifically, but to do a treatment which will simply support the process of change which is already underway. This treatment doesn't involve touching the knee itself at all. As this would seem odd without explanation, I start to tell him that I'm not going to work on the knee itself, but as soon as I start to explain, he interrupts me. He felt his knee change; he knows it is healing, and is happy to let it be.

What happened? Of course, I don't know for sure, but I have seen something similar so often now that I can make a good guess. If you were literally propping up a falling wall your knees would start to hurt under the strain (and then other parts of your body too). Even though the strain he was under wasn't physical, his body registered the strain, and registered it through an image he could grasp. So his symptom is a message, communicated not in language, because the body can't speak in words, but in an insistent and evocative pain in a particular place. It was communicating that if he carried on propping up the people in that company he would suffer for it. So when he made a promise to himself to stop doing that, the message had been received so the muscles could relax and the swelling start to subside. Although it took a few days for the knee to recover fully, recover it did.

This story suggests that symptoms are telling us something. Everyone knows that. If you've twisted an ankle, and it hurts, then it's telling you not to walk on it. But, for some reason, we tend to abandon this idea in the case of more complex symptoms. Hair loss in early middle age is put down to genes, migraines to periods, skin problems to allergic reactions. In other words they are regarded as simply some aberrant malfunction somewhere in the system, a kind of mechanical hiccup, which tells us nothing more than that we need to get an expert to fix it. But if you see illness as a consequence of imbalance, then symptoms become highly specific indicators of the nature of the imbalance, pointing us unerringly – if only we can understand that language – to what needs to be done to restore balance. Somewhat like dreams, they speak in their own language, communicating what the rational mind cannot grasp or is unwilling to hear.

The basic premise of all this is that if balance is restored, which may or may not need the active collaboration of the patient, the pain will go away, normal functioning will be restored, and the patient will get better. That seems like a belief in magic. Well, in a way it is, but not perhaps in the way you imagine.

> *As a surgeon I watch miracles daily ... the body knows much more than I do. In fact, every time I perform surgery I rely on its wisdom because I don't know how a wound heals or how anaesthesia works (nor does anyone else ...).*
>
> Bernie S. Siegel

For all Bernie Siegel's medical knowledge and skill, he knows that the way the body heals is still a mystery. Practitioners of any system of medicine can help it heal, but what they are doing, all they are doing, is catalyzing a healing reaction. The key question then becomes 'how best to stimulate that healing reaction?' In this light, it is at least plausible that when a person's energies are out of balance there isn't as much energy available to initiate or sustain healing.

Restoring balance

The different kinds of energy medicine use different techniques to restore balance – touch, colour, light, needles, herbs, and so on – and these techniques depend on particular ways of thinking about imbalance. Sometimes imbalance is seen in terms of opposites – like yin and yang, hard or soft tissue, weak or strong muscles, smooth or jerky rhythms – and restoring balance is essentially a matter of harmonizing those opposites. Sometimes it involves classifying people according to some kind of constitutional type – miasms in traditional homeopathy, tridosha in ayurvedic medicine, or elements in classical acupuncture – which predicts how a person of each type will typically become imbalanced and describes what he or she needs to do to restore balance. Instead of giving a very brief explanation of all of these, I am going to look at just one in more detail. I have chosen it partly because it has a wide application, forming the basis of certain styles of shiatsu, homeopathy, herbal medicine and acupuncture, and partly because it is the one I know best.

According to traditional Chinese medicine, human beings have five basic kinds of energy, and each of these needs to be balanced with the others. The five are as follows:

Wood energy

This is dynamic, forceful energy. It is the energy which powers the growth of trees and plants, especially the tremendous upward push of the seed from underground through the soil in springtime. It's the force that enables tree roots to break up concrete, and sends a rambler rose forty feet or more up a tree trunk and along its branches. In humans, this is the energy which can come up and out as anger. The shouting voice, the red face, the punched fist, the wagging finger, are all displays of this forceful energy.

Fire energy

This is the energy of summer – of warmth, intimacy and communication. It is the energy which enables us to relax and be joyful. Physically, the body needs to be kept warm to protect the functioning of the organs. Emotionally, each of us needs to feel warmth in at least some of our relationships with others. We need someone we can talk to who understands us, and we have a powerful need to give affection and love. This energy also goes upwards and outwards, but in a much gentler way than wood energy.

Earth energy

This is the energy of stability and fertility. You can see this energy at its zenith in the abundance of fruit on a plum tree or corn in the field at harvest time. It is strong in the kind of woman we call an 'earth mother', one who naturally nurtures, supports and provides. Its movement is circular, enfolding and protecting – the movement of a mother's arms holding a young baby at the breast. Mentally it can be the energy of worry, as the same thoughts go round and round without any resolution or outcome.

Metal energy

As you would expect, this energy has a sharp quality. It cuts away the inessential in order to find the desirable – the rare, the precious, the beautiful. It enables us to know the difference between real gold and fool's gold, recognizing and respecting what is truly valuable. In the natural world it is the energy of autumn, when leaves which have done their job fall and start to rot away while the seed is preserved. It is also the energy of grief: the emotion which helps us to appreciate what is really important and reminds us of our true values. It is a contraction and a concentration of energy.

Water energy

This is the energy of fluids, of ebb and flow, of waves and floods. It is the terrifying power of tidal surges, of rivers in spate. As water is essential for all life, its absence is just as frightening. When rivers dry up, or the water supply to a neighbourhood is cut off for days, people panic. They know, instinctively, that they can only live for a few days without water. Stagnant water is almost as bad as no water; it becomes polluted. A reliable steady flow is vital for well-being. The movement of this energy is downward, sinking.

These five are connected in two different ways. First, there is a cyclical pattern of creation – (Figure 4). Wood energy fuels fire, which nourishes earth, which generates metal, which gives rise to water, and so back to the start in an endless cycle of generation. You might call it a basic rhythm which sustains life. If each kind of energy is feeding the next one in the cycle properly, then each of them will have roughly the same amount of energy; they'll be balanced and the person will be well – or at least, sufficiently robust to recover easily from an illness. If a person falls ill, or can't get well again, then somewhere, somehow, this cycle will have broken down.

The other kind of connection is through control or restraint. Each kind of energy, as well as needing one other, also controls one other; it's a system of sticks as well as carrots (Figure 5).

In short, each kind of energy is maintained at an appropriate level partly by being fuelled, which makes sure it has enough, and partly by being restrained, which makes sure it doesn't have too much. The five work together; they are interdependent. So, on the one hand, if one of them is knocked away from its optimal level, there are forces which will help it return to normal: that is the body's natural resilience and ability to heal. One the other hand, it also means that if these forces aren't sufficiently strong, then the whole system will

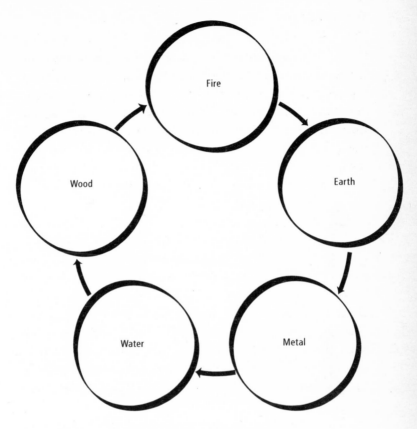

Figure 4: The arrows mean 'sustains', 'nourishes' or 'feeds'

suffer; that is when people are susceptible or can't seem to get well. All the different techniques of energy medicine aim, in one way or another, to help return the system to its state of balance. Here is one example to show how this theory works in practice:

A woman in her early thirties works as a cook. After some years in a restaurant, she decides to go freelance. She is very extrovert and sociable and has become well known in the

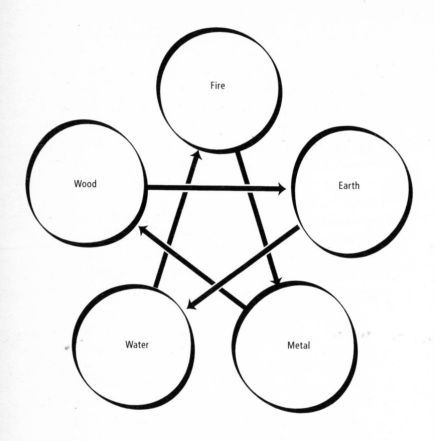

Figure 5: The arrows mean 'restains', 'inhibits' or 'controls'

entertainment world, so she will work for a few weeks cooking for a film crew on location or a group who are making a record at a studio. She gets hired not just for her cooking but also for the way she always has time to take care of anyone who is anxious or unhappy. After each bout of work she will then take a few weeks off. As her husband's work is freelance too, this suits them well – they normally manage to co-ordinate time at home and time away. They have been married for nearly ten years and are happy together.

For some time now she has been troubled with oedema. In her case, the main symptom is very swollen legs. There is a distinct bulge above her ankles, as if all the water in her body has dropped down to them and can't go any further. The swelling increases a bit when she ovulates. She has also had a number of lumps in her breasts, none of which have been malignant and which have been removed; she worries quite a bit that the next one will be cancerous. But the real reason she has come for treatment is that they both want to start a family. A couple of years ago she conceived twice but miscarried. Since then she hasn't been able to conceive at all. She loves children and is getting desperate. She tells me that she thinks it is this desperation which is making her so short-tempered. Previously she was pretty equable, but now she flies off the handle regularly and is quite shocked by the force of her anger once it is unleashed.

This woman's symptoms all point to the fact that her earth energy is very weak. That is the energy responsible for conception, and also for holding the foetus once it is conceived. If you look at Figure 5 you'll see that it is also responsible for controlling water energy, and that energy obviously isn't under control; the oedema in her legs and the lumps in her breasts are both a kind of flooding and a kind of stagnation. Finally, she is puzzled by how quick-tempered she has become recently. This points to the same conclusion. Excessive or inappropriate anger is the result of an over-abundance of wood energy; and so, of course, that energy is over-controlling her earth energy. I have represented all this in Figure 6.

Because I want, here, simply to explain energetic balance and imbalance, I'm not going to talk about the way a practitioner would check this initial diagnosis, nor about the next stages of pinning down precisely what has gone wrong, nor about how this imbalance could be treated. But simply thinking about this person in this way raises an interesting question. Given that her earth energy is so weak, it can't be getting sufficiently fed by her fire energy – the one before it in the creative cycle. Why not? I can't say anything conclusive about this, but there are possibilities well worth exploring. For one thing, she may be using all her fire energy to warm others and not keeping enough for herself; remember that she is 'very extrovert and sociable'. For another, it may be that all the nurturing she does for others by cooking for them, and generally supporting those in trouble, is an enormous drain on her earth energy, so however much her fire tries to feed it, earth can never get enough. It may be, in short, that helping her to see her symptoms in this way might enable her to make the kinds of changes in her life which would allow her to get well and to conceive.

There is an interesting refinement of this basic idea of imbalance between the different qualities of energy. Each kind of energy has, generally, two aspects, and they need to be in balance with each other. In the case of wood energy, for example, both aspects have the same forceful, outward, dynamic quality, but they have different functions. One operates long term and the other short term. Before describing how this works in human beings, you can see this division of functions in the way a tree grows. Within a beech nut is a blueprint which is different from the blueprint in an acorn. With that blueprint, the nut has to grow into a beech tree with its characteristic grey bark, leaves, and overall shape. That's the long-term aspect of wood energy. However, the blueprint doesn't determine exactly what the mature tree will look like; much depends on the environment in which it grows, the quality of the soil, the density of the trees around it, the rainfall in each year and so on. The shape taken by an individual tree depends on the tree's response to an endless variety of particular circumstances: that is the short-term aspect of wood energy.

Applying this idea to human beings, we need to have both an overall purpose, even a vision, of what we want to become. We also need to adapt to our environment and to respond

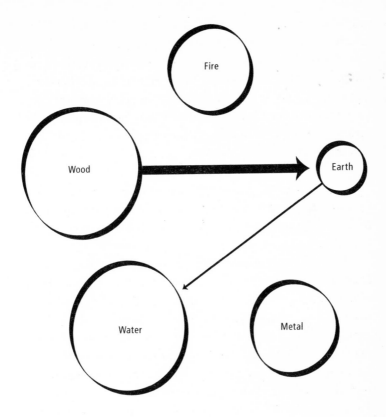

Figure 6: The size of the circles represents the amount of energy, and the size of the arrows the amount of flow between energies

quickly and skilfully to its changes. And, to do anything well, these two need to be in balance. I was once given a wonderful example of how they can get out of balance. In the course of interviewing a number of people who were making key decisions about nuclear weapons, one of them, probably the most influential, said to me 'and before we knew where we were, we looked round and suddenly we had two thousand tactical nuclear weapons in Europe that the generals had never asked for, the scientists didn't know what they did and the politicians didn't know what the hell they were for ...' In other words, there had been so many short-term decisions, specific responses to specific circumstances, that the overall purpose or plan had been forgotten. It's just as bad the other way round; wonderful plans are completely pointless without the detailed day-to-day decisions which are needed to implement them.

This example, and indeed this whole section, exemplifies one key idea common to all kinds of energy medicine. None of them sees illness as a specific thing which can be isolated and then defeated. Instead, they see illness as a state or condition of the system as a whole – as life not working well in a person. It is a person who is ill, not a part like a kidney, or a knee, or a function such as breathing or excretion, and help needs to be directed to helping the life in that system reassert itself. The same is true of what is conventionally called mental illness. If a person suffers from depression or has panic attacks, that will reveal itself throughout the system, irrespective of how we label the problem.

Finally, I want to return to the simplest instance of balance – the way we manage to balance on our feet. The sophisticated theory I have described in this section is all about inner functions, capacities, potentials; it isn't easy to see it in operation until you can see people and the way they behave as manifestations of these five energies; until you get into the habit of looking at them through these particular spectacles, so to speak. But it is very easy to see balance and imbalance in the way people stand, sit and walk. So many forms of illness stem from the way we stray from our natural structural balance, from the way we adopt instead rigid, artificial postures. This does not just apply to back pain, muscle spasms and joint problems. Holding our bodies in a state of imbalance also affects our organs, our circulation, our neurological and immunological networks. Correcting posture, helping it return to balance, is accordingly the basis of a huge range of recent techniques including Rolfing, Feldenkrais, Zero Balancing, and Alexander, as well as some very old ones such as Yoga and Tai Chi.

Illness and health

Although we all espouse the virtues and benefits of health, ironically it is a rather lifeless idea for most of us. What we really mean by it is the absence of illness. If there's nothing wrong with you, then you're healthy: and if you've been ill, healing means getting back to where you were beforehand. All this is rather negative, like saying we're at peace with someone just because we're not actually fighting. Both peace and health can have a much more powerful and positive meaning.

When a person is really well there's an unmistakable look to their skin, their eyes and their whole way of being with others. It is a kind of radiance. Some people have it although their lives may be difficult, and their work hard: they may even have it when they're in pain or coping with a disability. Others do not, even though they have every imaginable comfort. It isn't easy to say what it is. The best I can come up with is that the people who are healthy are living to their full potential, a potential which may have nothing whatever to do with worldly success. They also seem to know, and be accepting of, who they are and of what life has brought to them. Something like this is reflected in the state of those who have recovered from apparently fatal illnesses.

> *... the healing of the body for many was a byproduct of a new balance of mind and heart. It wasn't that these people felt better than ever because they had healed, but rather that they had healed because they had come upon a place of a bit more ease and peace within.*
>
> Stephen Levine

It is also borne out in this account of a meeting in the mountains on the borders of Nepal and Tibet.

The Llama of Crystal Mountain appears to be a very happy man, and yet I wonder how he feels about his isolation in the silences of Tsakang, which he has not left for eight years and now, because of his legs, may never leave again. Since Jang-bu seems uncomfortable with the Llama ... I tell him not to enquire on this point if it seems to him impertinent, but after a moment Jang-bu does so. And this holy man of great directness and simplicity, big white teeth shining, laughs out loud in an infectious way at Jang-bu's question. Indicating his twisted legs without a trace of self-pity or bitterness, as if they belonged to all of us, he casts his arms wide to the sky and the snow mountains, the high sun and the dancing sheep and cries 'Of course I'm happy here! It's wonderful! Especially when I have no choice!'

Peter Matthieson

These quotations suggest that the way we think about illness, cures, and health is too narrow. They take us back to the story of Pablo Casals at the start of this chapter. It is at least plausible to think that the very act of sitting at the piano and raising his hands to their well-known position, with the music he loves and wants to create already starting up in his head, restores balance in him. That playing is exactly what he needs now, in his old age, to be balanced. He isn't ill; he just functions less well when he is doing things which are less important to him. I said at the start of the chapter that illness may not be quite what we think it is; having arthritis when he isn't playing doesn't mean Pablo Casals is ill. You can see how a person might be well but still have twisted legs or arthritic hands. And you can see how the criterion of success we usually use for a successful medical intervention may be too narrow. A person may be healed in spite of the persistence of his or her ailments.

This may seem reasonable enough if the ailment is a minor inconvenience, but it sounds outrageous in the context of a serious or life-threatening illness. I know this from personal experience. I had a close friend who suffered from terminal cancer in early middle age, and I was shocked by what the illness did to her and what she had to go through. It would have been hard for me to accept that she might have been healed in spite of her illness. In a more religious age, or in other cultures which have a more spiritual view of life, it wouldn't be so difficult to talk about this issue. In such an age or culture, almost everyone would know what is meant by the soul; that is, some aspect of each person which is immortal. The body is born and dies, but the soul is eternal. Believing this, it is also easy to believe that the soul is much more fundamental than the body, and that it is implicated in what happens to us, irrespective of our wishes or intentions. Put bluntly, you might say that it has its own purposes and its own agenda. Of course, the conscious mind doesn't know what these are, so it may well rail against what the soul is choosing to do – especially in the case of serious illness. For those who see life in this way, then symptoms of serious illness may be more than messages from the mind or body which they can understand and act on appropriately: they may be the consequences of the soul's undertaking.

In this materialist age perhaps there is nothing I can say to the vast majority who don't believe in a soul or in any kind of transcendent power in the world. For them, suffering is simply awful and meaningless. But there are also plenty of people who at least trust that life is not random, and that we can be happy whatever it brings us and however tragic the circumstances – as the Llama of Crystal Mountain is happy. For them, healing may not mean getting rid of their ailments, may not mean getting better. They may even believe that a person can be healed even though he or she dies of an illness. This amounts to a faith that there is some deeper wisdom at work in the world. Einstein seems to have had this faith; in a different context he famously said, 'I refuse to believe that God plays dice with the world.'

Ram Dass, the spiritual teacher, has this kind of faith too. He suffered a debilitating stroke in his mid-sixties, and tells, with immense humour, the story of his reactions to it. First he was rather surprised that something like that should happen to such a spiritual person as himself. Next, as the all-pervading consequences of his disability began to become obvious, he tried to understand what it all meant; after all, he had spent decades helping those who were ill or dying and now, suddenly, he could neither speak nor move. Finally, beyond understanding, he saw that the life he had to lead from then on was a new kind of life, and one in which he could be happy. Then everything looked different, including his stroke. When he recovered the power of speech, albeit rather halting speech, he said he knew what had happened to him. He said, 'I was stroked'. Imagine being able to say that. What an extraordinary way of playing with the notion of what constitutes suffering and what constitutes healing. And although he will spend the rest of his life in a wheelchair, who could say that he is not healed?

What I am getting at is that to see illness as a physical malfunction may be to miss what is really important. Of course, none of us wants to be in pain or to be unable to live the life the fact that we are used to. But focusing on these things may be to overlook the fact that health is not the same as the absence of illness. I know people, I am sure you do too, who have no illness but sadly are in very poor health; and I am fortunate enough to have been inspired by knowing people who have an illness and are yet supremely healthy. Much of energy medicine is concerned to reduce pain and to restore people to their daily lives; but it doesn't stop there. It also aims to help a person become healthy, whatever that may mean for that particular individual and however it may manifest for him or her.

Chapter 3

Energy anatomy

All the experiments point to one unifying conclusion. The overall structure, the shape, the pattern, of any animal is as real a part of its body as are its cells, heart, limbs or teeth.

Robert O. Becker and Gary Selden

There are many well-known, but apparently inexplicable, symptoms which make perfect sense if you know a little about the organization of energy in the body. Here are three examples:

A lot of newborn babies have jaundice; clearly their livers don't start to work effectively as soon as they are born. But why should this be so? Why should the liver lag behind the kidneys or the spleen, for example? The answer isn't in the nature of the organ itself, but in its energy supply. The foetus gets its energy from its mother through the umbilical cord. As soon as it is born it starts to receive energy from its environment, and that energy is taken into the lungs first. From there it flows around the organs in a set sequence, fuelling each in turn. The liver is the last one in the cycle. So if the energy flow is a little slow to establish itself in a newborn baby and doesn't get right round the system quickly, the liver will be slow to start working properly. Hence the jaundice.

A high proportion of adults who suffer from chronic

asthma and bronchitis had skin complaints as children. The proportion is even higher if these skin complaints were sup-pressed by creams and ointments. If, as adults, these breathing difficulties are treated effectively and get better, what often happens is that the skin problems break out again, temporarily. Why should this be so? According to energy anatomy, the energy sub-system which nourishes the skin also supplies the lungs, so you would expect these two kinds of symptoms to be linked. More specifically, the childhood skin problems can be an early warning sign that all is not well in the lungs. Signs of mild distress in any organ are manifest first on the outside of the body, long before the organ itself is badly affected. If the real problem is ignored, for example by just applying creams to the skin, then the lungs will probably continue to deteriorate, and over time, the result may well be chronic asthma or bron-chitis. If these are treated and the lungs start to recover, then the skin complaints will reappear, briefly, as a sign of minor distress again on the way to health.

My last example is a well-known link between drinking coffee and chronic headaches which are on the side of the head; those who suffer from these kinds of headaches know that caffeine normally brings it on. Why should this be, and why should the headache be on just one part of the head? It's because caffeine affects the gall bladder particularly. If the gall bladder is under stress there will be a strain on the energy pathway that supplies the gall bladder, and it hurts. That pathway starts near the temples and covers the side of the head in a series of zig zags – and that's where the pain is felt.

It may seem a bit far-fetched to link the words anatomy and energy. The study of human anatomy in the West started with dissection; that was how people found out about the location and interrelationships of bones, muscles, organs and so on. When, in the Renaissance, artists started to attend and even carry out dissections, there was a dramatic change in the representation of the human body: it was no longer smooth and stylized; instead muscles rippled and bones protruded in just the way they would in a living person adopting the pose the artist was depicting in paint or marble. There was a dramatic change too in the medical view of the body. Dissection seemed to offer reliable knowledge about the body, so popular theories which postulated some 'vital spirit' or some tiny inner man, a homunculus, were confidently rejected on the reasonable grounds that none could be found in the cadaver. Accordingly, it was assumed, for a long time, that whatever was apparent from dissection was all there was to know. That assumption was shown to be wrong when the work of chemists in the 19th and 20th centuries revealed germs, enzymes, hormones, and so on. Oddly enough, however, some of the old assumption lingers. The idea that there is a complex and predictable organization of energy in the body is still dismissed on the grounds that nothing of that kind can be found in a dissected corpse. Indeed it can't, for the very simple reason that there isn't any organization of energy in a dead body. Energy is what animates us. By analogy, you won't pick up any television signals if the transmitter has gone dead.

Given a vast amount of clinical practice, over centuries, which is based on a common understanding of the location and functions of energy flows in the body, it seems sensible to make use of this knowledge, and most forms of energy medicine use it in one way or another. Again, I can't be comprehensive, and some of what follows will be tangential to some therapies: still, the basics are as important and as fascinating as the remarkable mechanics of the human skeleton.

Energy and structure

The energy flows of the body match the structure of the body; that is, they are closely associated with bone and muscle. Think of an energy flow as very like a flow of water. If you look at a stream or river, you will notice that where there is a sharp turn there are back eddies, little whirlpools, on the inside of the bend. Many of the acupuncture points in the body are like these whirlpools; they are places where the energy has slowed, collected. There is a bend on the inside of your knee, so, that's where you would expect to find acupuncture points, and indeed, there are four of them there. There's also one on the outside: I'll explain the reason for that in a moment. If you flex your wrist, to take another example, you'll find that you can bend it much further towards your body than away from it. There are three acupuncture points on the inside of the wrist, and only one on the back. You can also bend your wrist quite sharply to each side, and, as you'd expect, there is also an acupuncture point on each side of the wrist.

Using the analogy of a river again, you will notice that if there is a place where the bank juts out a bit you will see an eddy downstream; if it juts out a long way there will be eddies upstream too. Now, feel down the outside of your little finger from the tip towards the hand, and you will feel where bone juts out at the joint between finger and hand. Feel each side of that bony joint, pressing quite firmly, and you'll notice a slight indentation, a kind of soft hollow, on each side of it. Now, if you imagine a flow of energy coming down that finger, under the skin and alongside the bone, it would create eddies exactly in those hollows. That is where the acupuncture points are. You can do the same with the first finger; there are equivalent hollows and acupuncture points there too. The acupuncture points I mentioned on the outside of the knee and the wrist are formed like this; they are on the far side of a bump at the end of a bone.

The position of the chakras shows another aspect of the relationship of energy and bone. Chakra is a word in Hindi, usually translated as 'wheel'. It is something which is circular, turning and spinning, a vortex rather like the one formed in emptying bathwater as it spirals round the plug hole. In this context, they are vortices of energy rather like acupuncture points but much larger, each one having a particular quality and occupying a particular location in and around the body. Fritz Smith, a doctor, osteopath and acupuncturist, suddenly realized that they too followed the bone.

> *One day ... as I was lecturing on skeletal anatomy and pointing out the normal curves of the spine, it suddenly occurred to me that, as the current of energy flows through the spine and around the spinal bends, as I believe it does, vortices of energy would be created at the major curves. As I studied the skeleton and imagined these vortices whirling, I recalled the picture of a meditating yogi with the overlay of the spinal chakras, and instinctively I knew the chakras must exist. They were not just abstract symbols of an ancient religious system; they actually corresponded to the structure of the human skeletal system.*

> Fritz Frederick Smith

Figure 7 shows the location of the chakras in relation to the curves of the spine.

For many years I assumed that the energy flows simply followed the bone and muscles. That is, I assumed the structure was there first and the energy adapted itself to that structure. I now see that this assumption was typical of a Western view of the body, thinking of the material, the physical, as somehow primary. In the East the assumption is that the energy flows come first and that they organize the development of the bones and muscles. There is now some scientific evidence that this is true

A series of experiments was carried out on the embryos of chicks. In the chicks, energy pathways (called 'meridians' in what follows) were established within fifteen hours of conception – long before any of the organs started to be formed.

A doctor who has reviewed these experiments concluded:

> *Because the meridians become spatially organized within the embryo prior to the cells and organs finding their final positioning within the body, this would suggest that the meridian system provides a type of intermediate road map or informational guidance system to the developing cells of the body... Thus the organized energetic structure of the etheric body [what I have called the energy body] precedes and guides the development of the physical body.*

Richard Gerber

The point of all this is that many kinds of body pain and disability are seen as problems with the structure of the body, and surgery is used to correct the structure. If that works, well and good. But if it doesn't, people are often told that the operation wasn't a success and that they need another one. Repeated operations are not unusual. Instead, working with the energy flows through the structure may resolve the problem.

Seven months ago a man in his early sixties came to see me. He recently wrote to me about that first meeting, 'It's as well that we don't retain a memory of pain but I can remember being at desperation point, entirely sceptical, and not at all sure of what I was doing when I walked, staggered, into your care.' His lower back pain had lasted for five years, and hadn't got better in spite of osteopathic treatment and an operation to fuse vertebrae in his spine. His right leg had gone numb, and he had lost real control of his right foot, which he had to slap on the ground as he walked, rather as if he was wearing one flipper. The foot was cold, very white and somewhat deformed. The worst of it was that he could no longer sit at his desk, and he is a successful novelist with more books to write.

It didn't look as if manipulation of the structure would

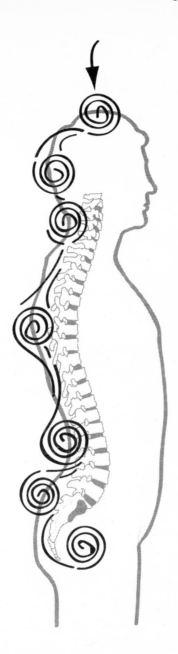

Figure 7

help; it hadn't worked, and in any case he wasn't willing to try any more of that. But if energy wasn't flowing properly through his structure, and could be helped to do so, perhaps the structure would respond. Certainly the state of his leg and foot suggested that there might be no proper flow of energy there – where there is energy the tissue is usually warm and has a good colour. As for his back, I remembered an old adage 'where there is no free flow there is pain' so there was a chance that there wasn't a free flow of energy in his back. Figure 8a gives a

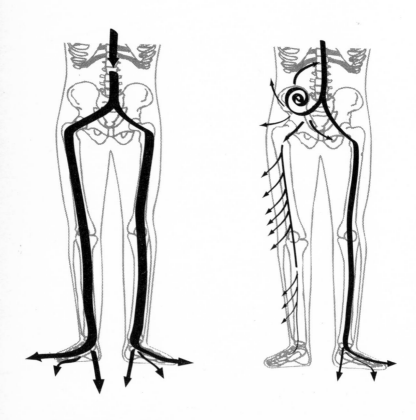

Figures 8A &B

rough idea of how energy should flow through the lower back, leg and foot and Figure 8b shows more or less what I found when I examined him. I didn't know, of course, if energy could be persuaded to flow again as it should, nor whether if it did so normal functioning would be restored. But he was willing to try, in spite of his scepticism: desperation has its uses.

There were ups and downs over the next seven months, but to his great credit he stuck with the treatment – in that time I treated him twelve times in all. The pain diminished considerably after the first treatment, and after three there was no pain in his back, but some in his foot. At that stage I asked him what he now wanted from the treatment, what would be his ideal outcome. Spreading his arms wide he practically shouted 'to be able to dance'. By the end, he had regained full sensation in his leg, his foot looked just like the other, and he walked normally. At his last session I put on an Irish jig, and he danced.

At the moment I am treating someone who has had three hip replacements in the same hip, and this latest one is now hurting. Clearly, whatever caused his hip to disintegrate in the first place has survived the operations and is still at work. It might be a disturbed or distorted energy flow. Again I don't know if re-establishing an appropriate flow of energy through that hip will allow the bone to maintain itself and support him without pain, but it is worth a try.

The organs and meridians

Bones and muscle provide one form of organization of the body; the organs provide another. Here again, there is an enormous difference between seeing things and seeing processes. Of course, the liver or the stomach or the colon is a separate identifiable part of the body, but it is also part of a process. The name of an organ, in energy medicine, refers to a process, to a general function which needs a particular kind of energy. That function and that energy is exemplified by a specific organ, but it isn't confined to that organ.

Take the colon for example. Essentially, the physical organ takes matter which the body doesn't need – dead cells and indigestible food – and excretes it. In energy terms, this is just one aspect of the whole business of elimination, of a natural, healthy and necessary impulse to let go. So childbirth is also seen as part of the function of the colon. This may seem very strange at first sight, but childbirth needs this kind of energy, and it needs huge amounts of it. Think of the tremendous shift in energy from the state of pregnancy to the drama of birth. During the whole of the nine months of pregnancy, earth energy is dominant in the mother in order to hold, support, nourish, and enclose the foetus. Suddenly, that energy has to be supplanted by a diametrically opposite energy – the energy of letting go and pushing away – and it takes a lot to do it. This is more than just a theory. Certain acupuncture points on the colon meridian will stimulate uterine contractions, and are routinely used to speed and ease childbirth; I used them on one of my own daughters in the labour ward. These points are so effective that they mustn't be used during pregnancy or there is a grave risk that they will induce a miscarriage.

At the physical level, if something is retained when it should be excreted it becomes toxic. The equivalent function at the mental level is letting go of ideas which have proved to be mistaken, plans which haven't worked, hopes unfulfilled, old loves, regrets, and a clinging to the memory of those who have died. Any of these, if retained for too long, can become toxic in the sense that they prevent a person from living life now and from creating new work and relationships. Miss Haversham in Great Expectations is a classic example, living in the wedding dress she wore on the day she was supposed to be married but was jilted. The same is true at what might be called the spiritual level. The sense of meaning in life, the kind of connection a person feels to something larger and more important than him or herself, changes as a person gets older. What matters most isn't the same at twenty as it is at fifty or seventy. Responding well to the process of aging involves letting go of some old beliefs, attitudes and values. The colon, seen energetically, is all about a willingness to change. It strikes me as true and helpful to look at change in this way. Not being able to let go of what is familiar and well understood, even if it is the source of pain and unhappiness, prevents people from adapting to new circumstances and moving on, even when they know that life would be better if they could.

All this casts a new light on symptoms of the colon like irritable bowel syndrome – a common complaint which does not always respond well to drugs. That may be because the drugs make no impact on an energy which is not working well, which holds on powerfully in the ways I have mentioned when it would normally let go. The irritation is a specific physical symptom of a specific kind of emotional, mental or spiritual distress.

Each organ, which, in energy medicine means the whole process or function of which that organ forms part, has a particularly close relationship with one other. In the case of the colon, its partner is the lungs. At first sight, this is surprising. I think immediately of the small intestine as the colon's natural partner; together they form one long tube from the stomach. But that, again, is to see the body through Western eyes. Energetically there are deep affinities between the lungs and colon. The lungs expel a waste product too – carbon dioxide. There is another parallel as well. The colon doesn't just excrete, it absorbs essential minerals and vitamins back into the body, rather as the lungs absorb essential oxygen into the blood stream.

In addition, the two organs work in tandem emotionally. Together they carry out the process of grieving. When people lose what has been loved, or even familiar, they need to grieve. When they are in that state their energy is taken up with letting go rather than taking in; typically, they lose an appetite for food. Similarly, someone in grief sighs and sobs, breathing with very small short in-breaths and big long out-breaths. The chest contracts as the lungs empty far more than is usual and, tends to become concave. When people start to recover from their grief they start to take in more air and regain the kind of forward-looking confidence which a full and open chest expresses. Taking in and letting go are two sides of the same coin. It is much easier to let go of the past if something is coming in to replace what was lost. Equally, it is much easier to bring new activities and relationships into your life if you make space for them by discontinuing the old ones – that is, if the colon is working well at letting go.

The colon and lungs work together because they have the same kind of energy. It is experienced as an inward, sinking, contracting energy. Sometimes we notice that a person in grief seems to have shrunk, to be physically smaller; that's because the energy body has been drawn in. Sometimes we say of the grief-stricken that they are hard to reach: I think this is the same phenomenon.

I could tell a similar story for each pair of organs, could set out their manifold aspects and their shared energies. But this example gives enough of a flavour of the whole so I want to turn now to another aspect of the interrelationships of the organs. At the start of this chapter I gave the example of jaundice in a newborn baby and said that energy flows around the organs in sequence, ending with the liver. Now there is time to elaborate on this idea of a sequence, I want to explain how it has two dimensions; one is in time and the other is in space: first time.

All the organs have a continuous energy supply, but for two specific hours every day each organ gets a boost. This boost is a bit like the Severn Bore, a single wave which moves up the estuary at a steady speed, passing towns and villages as it goes. Mostly we are unaware of this sequence through the body through one day and night; like flows of the lymph or peri-staltic contractions, it just does its own thing without needing any conscious instructions and without reporting back on how it's going. But if we regularly feel low and dispirited at a partic-ular time of day, then it may well be that all is not well with the organ which ought to be getting its boost just then. Feeling rotten is always worse if, by rights, you should be having a good time. For example, the organs which should be at their best from 7 to 9 pm and from 9 to 11 pm are fuelled by the energy of communication, of intimacy, and of companionship. That energy is working well in those big Italian families shouting at each other over a long dinner table loaded with food, all ages together, laughing and gossiping and teasing. If, at that time of day, all you really want to do is to be left alone with a cup of cocoa and a good book, chances are that those two organs aren't working well. You'll probably feel the cold easily too; in fact there will be all sorts of physical and emotional symptoms which, in one way or another, you'll be able to describe as lack of warmth.

There are lots of reasons why these organs might be suffer-ing, but a common one is a breakdown in the sequence. At the handover time, the organ before can't, or won't, let go of the energy it has had; or the organ which is supposed to pick it up next can't manage to do it. When this happens you usually know about it, partly because the timing is so very specific and partly because you can't explain what is happening. You might come over dizzy, or nauseous, suddenly have to sit down, or, if the changeover time is in the night, you'll wake up. A lot of people wake at 3 am regularly; that time is the end of one complete cycle, when the last organ in the cycle, the liver, has had its two hour boost and passes it on to the lungs, which simultaneously receive a fresh input of energy and set the whole sequence off again. So, if you've had a lot of alcohol in the evening you might wake then. The liver has been working like mad dealing with the booze, and it hasn't been able to finish the job, so it doesn't let go of its boost when its time is up. The lungs complain so vociferously that they wake you up.

Now for the sequence in space. The meridians flow along particular parts of the body; Figure 9 shows the location of some of them.

As you will see from the figure, the end of one meridian isn't in exactly the same place as the start of the next one in the cycle. What normally happens is that as the energy comes to the end of one meridian it joins up easily with the start of the next one. But sometimes it doesn't get passed from one meridian to the next – somewhat like a dropped baton in a relay race. Consequently the organ which is fed by that second meridian will be starved, sending out distress signals in the form of symptoms. Often, too, there will be some pain or discomfort quite precisely at the first point of its meridian. A very common example is an itch or an ache right in the corner of the eye, nearest the nose. That's because it's the location of the first point of the bladder meridian, so it is signalling that it isn't getting energy from the one before it in the cycle. That's the small intestine meridian. One of the functions of the small intestine is to sort out what is good for the system and what isn't, and to keep out or neutralize anything harmful. It deals, for example with pollen; and if a person is particularly susceptible to pollen it has an enormous job on its hands in late spring and early summer. Under strain, it tends not to pass energy on to the next meridian in the cycle, the bladder meridian. That's why many people who suffer from hay fever find that point in the corner of the eye irritated and irritating; it's the first point of the bladder meridian and it isn't getting its supply. And because that point provides the energy which regulates fluid levels in the eye, the eyes either get very dry or very runny – or, most often, wobble alarmingly between the two. All classic symptoms of what we call hay fever.

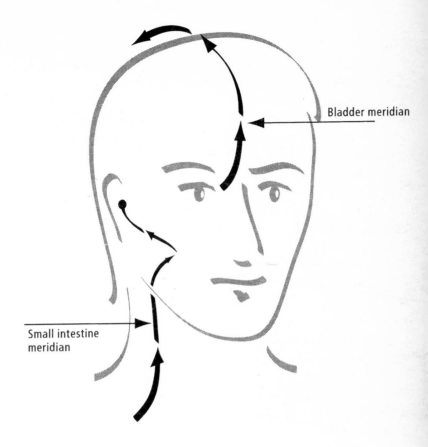

Bladder meridian

Small intestine
meridian

Figure 9

Movement

The body doesn't stay still very often nor for very long – even
when you're asleep in bed at night, there's a lot of twitching
and changes of position, and the trunk moves with every
breath. Movement both takes energy and also directs energy
through the body. Scientifically speaking, when you walk, or
pick up a pan, that creates a stress on your bones, which in turn
generates an electrical current in those bones (technically

known as piezoelectricity). Energetically speaking, movement sends energy through the bone in highly specific ways. Whichever way you look at it, movement helps bones to grow, and grow in the right shape – which is why exercise is so important to prevent osteoporosis.

It is second nature to swing your arms as you walk. You may have noticed that you swing them in a very particular way: as the left foot hits the ground the right hand reaches the top of its swing – and vice versa. Try making your right hand swing forward at the same time as your right foot hits the ground; it's quite hard to do and it feels really weird. What's going on is that walking creates a flow of energy through the body which has roughly the same shape as a figure of eight (Figure 10a). The flow is up along one leg, through the sacroiliac joint to the shoulder on the opposite side. It goes both up and down at the same time. The shoulder seems to initiate the movement, which will send energy down, and the pressure of the foot landing will send energy back up again. As it is all one movement it is hard to say whether it really starts in the foot or the shoulder; it's chicken and egg. Also, because there is also movement from side to side, the real shape of the energy flow is more like an hourglass than a figure of eight (Figure 10b).

The point of all this is that it explains some common complaints and shows how they can be treated. For one thing, if a person has a problem in one foot then it will almost always have affected the opposite shoulder. Treating the foot will help, but to make a real difference the shoulder will need to be treated as well. And, of course, if a person has a shoulder problem, the opposite foot will probably need attention.

And so often when people have difficulty walking – their feet or knees or hips are stiff and painful – the real problem is in the sacroiliac joint. As you can see from Figure 10, all the energy funnels into that area. If energy isn't flowing well through that energetic bottleneck, then all the other joints involved in walking will be suffering and complaining. To try and get the feet, the knees or the hips right while energy isn't flowing properly through the sacroiliac joint is like trying to get a car started by cleaning the carburettor (or even replacing it) when there is a blockage in the fuel pipe.

These energy flows engendered by movement interact with all the others – and the resulting picture can be very complex.

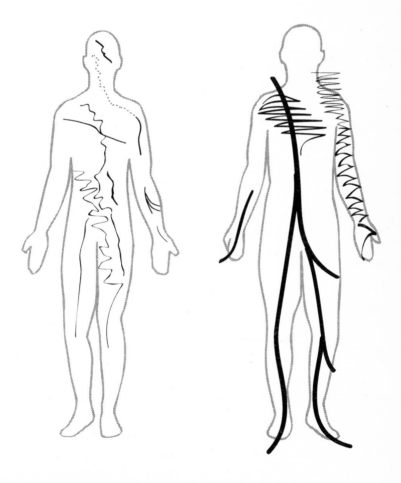

Figure 10a   Figure 10b

I want to take one example to show how understanding these different flows can lead to a useful diagnosis of a problem which is both common and difficult to treat.

Shoulder problems often come on for no apparent reason and they can take a long time to get better. They nearly all involve some difficulty in moving the shoulder blade. The reason for this is that all but the tiniest motion of the arm involves a movement of the shoulder blade too. You can try this for yourself by putting one hand on the shoulder blade on the opposite side of your body – you'll need to put your arm round the front of your neck to reach it. With that hand in place, try moving the other arm a little and you'll feel the response in the shoulder blade. With big motions of the arm it has to move a long way. Watch someone push his arms back like a soldier on parade and then hug himself, and you'll see this clearly. If the shoulder blade isn't floating freely on top of the ribs then, as you move your arm, the shoulder blade will be inhibiting the movement, pulling against it. There may be a simple explanation why this is happening, and an easy remedy. But often there isn't, and it helps to look at energy anatomy.

As I've just mentioned, the first place to look for the source of the problem is the opposite foot and the sacroiliac joint; if energy isn't flowing properly through them then, whatever else might help the shoulder, it won't get better quickly or easily until those flows are restored. Next, the small intestine meridian runs up the back of the arm into the shoulder joint. It penetrates the place where three bones meet, and from there it flows across the shoulder blade in a zig zag. Hence, the small intestine is intimately connected with the shoulder (there are two other meridians which also cross the shoulder, but I'll ignore them for the sake of this example). If the organ is in distress, then that distress will be manifested along its meridian. As always, problems show up externally before they become severe internally. These external signs are like early warning lights on the dashboard of a car: and the consequences of ignoring them are similar too.

So the next step is to investigate the state of the small intestine. The practitioner will ask questions about what was happening in the patient's life at the time the shoulder problems started. Did he suddenly start to have allergic reactions to certain foods? Was his life style harming him physically or mentally, for example by eating lots of junk food or by working in an organization which required him to act in ways he found unethical? Was he facing changes in his life and finding it difficult to decide what he really wanted? All these questions are directed at discovering if the small intestine was under the kind of pressure which might cause it to falter. If it was, then treating it will almost certainly help the shoulder to heal.

The protective layer

Bone carries the deepest flows of energy in the body. The meridians are nearer the surface, in the soft tissue. Then there is another kind of energy just under the skin. Although this energy also has flows, it is easiest to think of it as a sort of sheath which envelops the whole body in an unbroken layer. Its function is to provide protection from the environment.

Some of the protection we need is pretty obvious – excessive heat or cold can be dangerous because the organs need to be kept at a steady temperature and within a fairly narrow range. Damp can harm the lungs, draughts give us colds, and so on. I'm sure you know the feeling when this layer has cracked under the strain; you've felt the cold get right into you, somehow, or you've got so hot that you can't bear to be in the sun the next day. I know that, for me, this layer is weak on my upper back. If there is a draught anywhere else on my body I can sit in it all day and hardly notice it; but if the draught is on my upper back I quickly feel very uncomfortable, and if I have to sit in it for an hour or so, I get a cold. Those who are vulnerable to illness, who pick up whatever is flying around, probably have a weakness, maybe even a hole, in this protective layer.

Less obviously, and thanks to the pioneering research by Robert Becker, there is plenty of evidence that the body is affected by electricity. Electrical appliances give off energy, and if the body's protective layer isn't strong enough to resist and repel that energy, it can disrupt internal systems quite severely. Not much is known about the specific effects of this so-called electromagnetic pollution, but there is no doubt that some people can be badly affected by it.

Probably more significant for most people are the effects of the energies of those with whom they spend a lot of time – their families, work colleagues and close friends. As is well known, the menstrual rhythms of women who live together, or even spend a lot of time at work together, tend to synchronize. This is an energetic phenomenon. In physics it is known as entraining. Where two things are in close proximity, and both are in a regular movement, then over time they will end up moving in the same way at the same time. You might say that they fall into line with each other.

The same thing happens with emotional states. An emotional state is an energetic phenomenon too – indeed the word emotion means, literally, movement away from. Each emotion has its own distinctive pattern of energy. And the point is that if you spend a lot of time with someone in one of these states, its energy is quite contagious. It is genuinely difficult to stay calm, kindly and patient in the presence of someone who is very angry, and it is hard to be optimistic and dynamic if you live with someone who is depressed. The stronger the layer of protective energy, the easier it is to resist being swept up in the emotional state of another person.

A person's energy is also affected by what psychologists call projection. The idea behind this is that we each have the potential to be anything, but we are only conscious of a small part of this potential; the rest hasn't gone away, it is still there, but we aren't aware of it. So a banker, for example, has the potential to be a drop-out, a monogamous person to be promiscuous, a saint to be a murderer, and vice versa. Unwilling to recognize or accept that aspect of ourselves, we see it in others instead, and react. Usually we react with horror because, most often, what we don't recognize in ourselves is something we don't want to recognize, don't believe we have; indeed is something we deplore. Projection is the power behind prejudice and pogroms. It can sometimes work the other way and lead us to uncritical adulation; the other has some quality we admire hugely but don't believe we have ourselves. This is the power behind the veneration of cult leaders, film stars and even one's own partner in the early days of falling in love. The word projection comes from cinema; the image on the film is projected on to a screen, and we see it there.

So if your father, for example, projects his own clumsiness, disorganization and irresponsibility onto you, that's a kind of energy coming at you. If your protective layer is strong and well, it'll just bounce off. But if it isn't and you don't notice the projection quickly enough to resist it consciously, it will have an effect – you'll probably start dropping things and losing your keys; things you don't normally do, and things you stop doing when you're not together.

All this is to say that our bodies can be affected by the environment – natural, artificial, and interpersonal – in which we live. These kinds of influences can wreak powerful changes. Allowing some disruptive energy to get into the body over and over again is a recipe for physical problems later – and by the time the invasion manifests itself in physical symptoms, the road back to health can be long and difficult. Energy medicine can help to mend, maintain, and enhance the strength of the protective layer. As with any problem, prevention is better than cure.

The whole

Although I have talked about a few of the ways in which energy is organized in the human body, the reality is far more complex. For one thing, there are many other flows which I haven't mentioned. For another, these aspects of energy anatomy are not separate and in the case of any trauma, injury or serious illness, all of them will be involved in some way. Instead of trying to list and describe all these flows and interconnections, I want to end with the example of breathing, which is fundamental not only to survival but to living life to the full.

First, breathing and physiology are intimately connected. Getting more air into the lungs, and getting it moving faster, is going to have an affect on cell chemistry throughout the body, and affect it for the better. Next there is the relationship between breathing and body structure. Dr Sutherland, who set cranial osteopathy on a firm footing, realized that the entire spinal column was involved in breathing. On an in-breath, the base of the sacrum goes back, and it comes forward again on an out-breath. At the same time, and co-ordinated with this rocking movement, the bones of the skull move in relation to each other. All these movements serve to pump cerebro-spinal fluid up the spine, around the brain, and back down again in a pulsing rhythm, which anyone can learn to feel quite distinctly. And the musculature of the body is involved in every breath too – most obviously the diaphragm, but also the muscles of the chest as most of the ribs lift, move outwards, and rotate along their axis.

What has all this to do with energy? To answer that question, here is a story of an energy medicine treatment, told by a journalist writing in *The Times*:

> *Somewhere in the mists of time there is a memory of a*
> *young and frantic mother rushing her choking baby to*

hospital. It is 1960, so the scenario is more Dr Kildare than high-tech ER. Everyone knows, including the distraught mother, that this is advanced pneumonia and the chances of survival are slim.

It is impossible to feed or to administer drugs orally to the baby girl, so deep surgical wounds are made at the top of her thigh, around her ankles and at the back of her knees to insert the IV drips. She beats the odds and lives ...

Here in the West ... we assume that the physical recovery is the end of the matter, especially with a young child who has no conscious memory of these events and whose only reminder are the physical scars from the feeding tubes.

That was what I thought too – until I put myself in the hands, literally, of the American physician who has created a potent and little-known technique called zero balancing. I discovered that the near-death incident that I had experienced when I was six months old had left a legacy of more than scarred tissue. It had fundamentally changed the way that I breathe.

What was clear to Dr Fritz Smith – and what I also came to understand ... was that this memory, far from fading, was encoded in the deepest recesses of my body, skeleton and energy fields, and was still affecting me 39 years later ...

During our session I felt deeply relaxed until Dr Smith asked me to breathe into the area below the clavicle where he was creating a fulcrum with his fingers. I tried and failed. I tried again and felt as if I were

*pushing a concrete ball up a steep hill. Starting to feel
stressed and panicky, I tried once more and
eventually felt the energy struggle through the top of
my chest. I had succeeded, but at a price.*

*As I did this, I felt the most awful lump in my throat.
The kind you get when you wake in the morning and
remember that your best friend has died. What I felt
was an overwhelming sadness ...*

*Dr Smith said he did not know me well enough to
interpret this energy block but that it had lodged there
as a reaction to some childhood illness or problem.
As he said this, I remembered the scars from the
pneumonia and the illness of which I have no
conscious memory. 'Try to practise breathing from up
here. Your lungs will thank you,' he advised.*

Susan Clark

This is a dramatic story, and one which may seem far removed
from normal life, but most people have had some traumatic
experience which has left its mark on the energy body. And it
does illustrate the fundamental interconnection between a
person's energy and structure. Dr Smith, touching underlying
bone with his hands (that's what 'creating a fulcrum with his
fingers' means), enabled Susan to realize first that she couldn't
get her rib cage to expand to enable her to breathe in the upper
part of her lungs, and second to feel 'the energy struggle
through the top of my chest'. It goes deeper than this too.
Susan Clark didn't realize that her breathing was inhibited; nor
did she realize that she was holding overwhelming sadness in
her body. As she started to change the mechanics of her
breathing, long forgotten feelings surfaced; so there must also
be a connection between structure, energy and emotion. With

a change in something as fundamental as breathing, there will be changes in the whole person whether or not we choose to see its parts and systems as separate.

There are other fascinating aspects to Susan Clark's story as well. How did Dr Smith know where to put his hands? How did he know to ask her to breathe into her upper chest? How did those two things together create such a powerful effect? And, most remarkable of all, how did he know, through touch alone, that her energy block 'had lodged there as a reaction to some childhood illness or problem'? The answer to these questions lies in a lifetime of experience of working with energy and years of reflection on clinical practice. But the following chapters will show, at least in principle, how it is done.

Chapter 4

Sensing imbalance

*It is more important for the doctor
to know the patient who has the disease
than to know the disease that has
the patient.*

Dr Albert Schweitzer

At this point in the book there is a shift of perspective. So far, I have looked at the basic premises of energy medicine, its view of the body and its ailments. In the next three chapters I look at the practicalities – finding out what might be the matter and putting it right. This is a complex process involving diagnosis, forms of treatment, evaluation of outcomes, and a continuing relationship between a patient and a practitioner. All these are interwoven. You do start to feel better if someone with real expertise and experience is paying close attention to you and your complaints. And most initial diagnoses need to be tested and refined by judging how well you respond to treatment based on that initial diagnosis: Did the treatment have the predicted results? Is your recovery slower than expected? Did you have any troublesome side effects?

Part of this shift of perspective is looking at the whole process from the point of view of the practitioner. You already know what it is like to be a patient, of some form of medicine at any rate.   If you are anything like me, you've felt a strange mixture of anxiety, powerlessness, hope, trust, gratitude, and sometimes disillusion.   What you probably don't know is what this complex process looks like from the point of view of the practitioner, and to understand how energy medicine works you need to know what your practitioner is doing and why he or she is doing it.   The process starts with diagnosis.

The heading quotation, from one of the most famous physicians of the twentieth century, has a nice ring to it. It is easy to agree that it is a terribly good idea, and it is also easy then to ignore it. No doubt there are all sorts of practical difficulties about getting to know the patient – there isn't enough time, most of them don't come very often, and so on – but more important than any of these is a belief that it isn't what really matters. According to this belief, getting to know the patient is an optional extra, an agreeable bonus, but it is no substitute for finding out what is wrong. What is wrong must be something like a virus, a growth, a blood clot, a torn muscle, a missing hormone, a constricted airway. In order to help the patient, the first step is to identify the thing that is causing the problem. That's the point of diagnosis.

You can't find what's wrong unless you have an idea of what to look for. If your computer doesn't start when you switch it on, you look to see if it is plugged in. That is the first, and most obvious, diagnosis of the problem. If you're like me, and you find that it is plugged in but still doesn't work, then you're baffled. You don't know where else to look. If you understand computers, of course, you'll be able to think of all sorts of other places to look, because you know what might not be working. In other words, any diagnosis depends on knowing what can go wrong. When a doctor examines a patient, she has some knowledge of a wide range of illnesses and diseases. Diabetes Mellitus or Crohn's disease are classifications of ways in which particular parts of the body can go wrong. Given a patient's symptoms and a knowledge of diseases, the doctor has a rough idea of where to look for what might be wrong; then she gets tests done to narrow the search and eliminate various possibilities until finally, with a bit of luck, she finds a match between one classification and the state of the patient. Then she says 'it's Diabetes Mellitus' or 'Crohn's disease'. The rest is plain sailing. Diabetes Mellitus or Crohn's disease are well understood, and there are obvious and appropriate treatments for them.

All this is perfectly sensible and it is done countless times every day. But this brief description of how diagnosis is done leaves out what Dr Schweitzer, speaking from the experience of a lifetime of medical practice, insists is vital: that is, knowing the patient. What can he mean?

I'm sure he had a lot of aspects of healing in mind, but the one I want to look at here is rooted in the fact that we are both all alike and all different. The classification of illness and disease is based on us all being alike; we all need insulin and if we don't have enough then there will be wholly pre-dictable consequences, which we call Diabetes Mellitus. That's one level of diagnosis. Digging a little deeper, we can also say that for everyone who has this illness there must be something amiss with the pancreas, because that is what produces the right quantity of insulin if it is working properly. But at the next level down, if we ask why the pancreas isn't working properly, we can't say anything which holds good for everyone. There are a limitless number of possibilities, and that is because we are all different. Then the diagnostic question changes. As we can no longer ask, 'in what way are all these people the same?' we have to ask, 'why is this person different and why is this particular pancreas in this particular person not working properly?' To begin to answer that question, the doctor does indeed have to know the patient. I have used the example of Diabetes Mellitus, but the point holds good for any illness.

It is the same with energy. Each of us has an energy body

which has a basic structure and a basic way of functioning which is the same as everyone else's: yet at the same time each person's energy body is unique. Sometimes the patient's energy body is so obviously out of balance that the practitioner need look no further than the basics in order to make a diagnosis that will help, at least in the short term. But much more often the exact nature of the imbalance isn't obvious, or it becomes clear that the obvious imbalance is really the consequence of some deeper and less apparent problem. And the more the practitioner learns about the patient, the more his imbalance seems unique: not dissimilar to plenty of others which the practitioner has seen, but somehow with its own shape and quality and its own way of being unable to right itself. In all these cases the only route to a useful diagnosis is through seeing the patient's individuality. It's another aspect of the issue discussed in Chapter 2 – that a patient's illness has meaning. Diagnosis then becomes a matter of getting to know the patient in order to get to know his disease.

Getting to know the patient isn't a matter of social chit chat. My children always knew when I was about to get angry; it wasn't until they were grown up, and the information was no longer useful, that they were willing to tell me how they knew. Apparently my nose sort of twisted and got a funny white patch on it. They knew this because they paid close attention; when you're young, it is very useful to have advance warning of when your father is about to get angry – you can make yourself scarce. Similarly, if a practitioner pays the closest possible attention to the state of the patient's energy body she will come to understand both the way that body and all its invisible systems work when all is well, and the particular individual way they are failing to work properly. That comparison will point to the quick route back to health.

People give out clues the whole time. This is a quotation from a newspaper article:

*When Carol Rayman's hair began to fall out, she felt
beside herself. 'I could not face the thought of going
bald,' says Carol, who is in her fifties ... An eminent
dermatologist relieved her of £1,000, told her she had
'male-pattern baldness' and suggested she go and buy
a wig. 'I thought of holidays and imagined the wig
floating off to sea. Going bald takes every bit of
femininity away from you. I am a big-hair person.
I felt so miserable.'*

Barbara Lentell

Even in this tiny extract, Carol is giving an enormous
amount of information about her energy body. She is explaining that it is normally expanded and dynamic, 'I am a big-
hair person'. By adding 'I felt so miserable' and 'I could not
face the thought ...' she is also saying that now it has become
contracted, dense and tight. We know too that she normally
likes to make a joke of things – '... the wig floating off to sea'.
This has two distinct implications. First, that establishing a
good mutual understanding of her condition won't be easy.
That's because on the one hand, Carol likes to treat things
lightly and to make fun of herself and her predicament, and
on the other, her hair loss is a serious matter for her.
Somehow, in the process of diagnosis, the practitioner has to
give credence to both of these at once. Second, the joking
shows that there is plenty of her normal healthy energy to
work with; the prognosis is good.

And as the dialogue develops the practitioner will notice
how the patient's energy body changes as the conversation
ranges over topics which are comfortable to discuss and those
which are difficult. It may also change in response to the
growing intimacy between them. This act of noticing sounds
passive; it is anything but. Paying really close attention to
another human being has a profound effect on him or her. I

will say more about this later, but first I need to explain how a practitioner diagnoses the state of the energy body. It is done by using all the senses, except the sense of taste.

Sight

Practitioners learn a lot just from watching the patient walking into the room. The shape of the body tells a story. There are overall qualities like fat or thin, wiry or relaxed, quick or slow, and there are often fascinating disjunctions. One person has a large upper body and you expect him to have stocky legs to support it; in fact they are thin and splay out uncertainly as he walks. Another talks very quickly and fluently but moves with very rigid, almost clockwork movements. Posture tells a story too.

> Watch a child carefully: you'll see that he seems to move with an outer layer of his body. His bones don't seem to be stabilized. Children go on in this way until they get to adolescence. They operate on what we call extrinsic muscles; this makes for the incoordinations which we associate with children ... The random, unbalanced adult individual may also be operating almost exclusively with external muscles. He has not grown up. He is using his body as if it were a child's body, and this will reflect in his emotional behavior as well ... You don't have to see the whole man. Every move he makes tells you what his structure is. You have only to have one local joint movement to tell you what is wrong with the whole guy. Could be the toe, could be the ankle, or the knee, or the head. Because, you see, if one part has changed this way, the next must have changed that way, and so forth.
>
> Ida Rolf

The practitioner will also notice the patient's colour. This is a large subject and I can only mention a few aspects of it here. There is usually an overall colour on the face and often a different colour in some key places – at the temples, in the lines which run from the side of the nose to the corners of the mouth, under the eyes, around the mouth. These colours give an excellent indication of which functions, and their associated organs, are in distress: a bluey-black colour points to the kidneys, yellow to the spleen, green to the liver and so on. It isn't quite as simple as it sounds because often the colours are mixed; if the kidneys and spleen are both under stress, then the colour may be a sort of muddy brown or the sort of green you get from combining blue and yellow, and that green has to be distinguished from the green which comes from the liver.

In addition, the patient's colour will change in the course of diagnosis and treatment, and the change gives valuable clues as to what is happening inside. Again disjunctions are particularly revealing. Imagine a patient who comes for treatment for a chest complaint which won't clear up. His face is a normal colour, perhaps a little more pink than most. He talks about how he has been having a difficult time; as well as being under the weather physically, he has been making mistakes at work, and one of his teenage children was recently caught in possession of cannabis. He says all this in a very matter-of-fact way, as if it is just part of normal life. Then he adds, 'and in the middle of it all I had to take a day off work because our dog became very ill and I had to take him to the vet to be put down.' The words have the same neutral quality, but the practitioner notices that as he says them his face goes white. That is a sure sign of grief. The death of the dog may have hit him harder than he realized, but much more likely is that he is grieving the loss of other things – perhaps his reputation and status at work, his children growing up and away – and he has not admitted this to himself. It is only when talking about a death that this grief is contacted and is unwittingly revealed.

As I explained earlier, grief typically contracts the energy body, especially in the chest area, so it is likely that his chest complaint is the physical symptom of his unacknowledged and unexpressed grief. The colour change was the key diagnostic clue.

To an experienced eye, the state of practically any part of the body will tell a story about what is going on inside. Some practitioners diagnose mainly by looking closely at each part of the eye, others by the state of the tongue. This requires keen observation. The tongue, for example, has an overall shape, colour, coating and moistness: four pieces of information there. And there may be differences in the colour at the sides, the middle or the tip; such differences will convey more information – and the same applies, of course, to coating and moistness. As you can see, the number of combinations is enormous and allows for a pretty fine discrimination of illness.

In general, the point is that every part of the body reflects the state of the whole; as Ida Rolf puts it, 'if one part has changed this way, the next must have changed that way'. The seen reveals the unseen. More specifically, the appearance of a particular external part conveys information about an inner state. The tip of the tongue, for example, corresponds to the heart, white on the skin of the temples to grief, and so on. These correspondence aren't theoretical; they are the result of careful observation by skilled practitioners in many different cultures over hundreds, even thousands, of years who have all come to the same conclusion. In that sense they are purely scientific.

Touch

The use of touch in diagnosis is just the refinement of a normal human skill. Most mothers can tell if their baby isn't well by touching its skin; it will feel clammy or rough or in some other way different from normal. Practitioners can do this too and the better ones can use the information conveyed by the skin to pinpoint an illness and to tell whether or not a particular treatment is working. In some forms of medicine, especially Japanese ones, the skill of feeling the abdomen or feeling along the lines of the meridians has been raised to a high art. Many osteopaths, chiropractors and zero balancers can diagnose through touching bone – they have developed a sensitivity to how a bone should feel when it is functioning well and can distinguish different kinds of dysfunction from their characteristic effects on the surface of a bone. Reflexologists know which organs are in distress through the feeling of the skin and tissue of particular areas of the foot. And as well as these specific skills, most practitioners learn a lot if there is any dissonance between the physical body and the energy body. I once treated a young girl, who was slim and fit and light on her feet. She lay down on the treatment couch and I lifted her legs a few inches off the couch. They were light; they weighed more or less what I expected from looking at her. I then put my hands under her back and lifted it a little. It was quite a shock. It was so heavy it was a real effort to lift it at all; it felt like the torso of a well-built forty-year-old man. There was something not at all well with the energy of her upper body.

I have mentioned all these varieties of touch quite briefly because there is one form of touch which I want to describe in more detail: it yields a wealth of reliable diagnostic information. It is touch on the patient's pulse.

The pulse is the rhythmic expansion and contraction of an artery as blood is pumped through it by the heart. The easiest place to feel the pulse is on the inside of the wrist, about an inch from the base of the thumb and just below the upper bone of the arm. You can feel it quite easily on yourself, though you may have to search around a bit to get the fingertip right on it. Then you'll feel the beat as your skin is pushed up towards your fingertip. As everyone knows, feeling the pulse and counting how many times it beats in a minute is a way of measuring the heart rate. That can be useful diagnostic information, but there is vastly more to be learned from the pulse.

What was discovered in the East, thousands of years ago, is that the pulse often feels a bit different if you put your fingertip a little nearer or further from the thumb, along the artery. In one place it may feel stronger than in another. Or it may be that in one place it feels slippery – as if you are putting your fingertip on a ball bearing – but in another it is sharp and wiry. No doubt many people have noticed this over the years and said to themselves 'that's funny', and never given it another thought. Luckily, plenty of practitioners did investigate this phenomenon, and they came to agree on what these variations mean. Summarizing, there are three places on each wrist where the strength and quality of the pulse can be distinguished; and in each of those places the pulse may feel different if it is touched lightly or firmly. This gives a total of twelve different pulses and twelve different places to feel them. And, again no doubt through centuries of trial and error, they discovered that each of these twelve pulses gives a very accurate read-out of the state of a particular function of the body and its associated organ. For example, there is a pulse which reflects the state of the energy of the colon. Properly understood, that will tell you how the colon as an organ is working, whether it is constipated, or the stool is too loose, whether minerals are being reabsorbed properly or there is inflammation in the lining. It will also tell you about how easy it is for the patient to deal with the whole business of letting go of what doesn't nourish or sustain him: old resentments and grievances, lost opportunities, or believing that only with a former lover can he be happy.

When I first started to study acupuncture I knew the theory but I doubted whether touching a particular pulse really did give reliable information. Then one day I took the pulses of one of my daughters. Eleven of them weren't quite the same as usual and the twelfth was very, very different: it was much fuller and stronger than before – my finger felt as if it was on a bouncy castle. I remembered from my training that this was how the pulse of a pregnant woman was described. It was quite a shock (especially as she hadn't told me). I didn't say anything. I wasn't sure, and anyway who wants her father to tell her she is pregnant? Six weeks later she told me. At the time I had taken the pulse she was indeed pregnant, but it was so early on that she hadn't known it herself. That convinced me of the accuracy of pulses.

Although beginners can pick up a lot of basic information from the pulses, it takes a lifetime to learn how to gather all the information they contain. Not only can the strength of each pulse vary enormously, and each degree of strength tell a different story, but a pulse also has what is called a quality; that is a specific kind of feeling to it. 'Slippery', mentioned above is one such quality, 'knotted' and 'scattered' are others. These words are simply attempts to describe the sensation of the pulse under the fingertips. Traditionally, there are said to be twenty-eight possible qualities, but that is just a classification and an experienced practitioner will be aware of many more. So each individual pulse communicates a wealth of information about the state of the organ and the workings of the function represented by that organ.

But that is still only a small part of the picture. If an organization had twelve people working for it, and things were going wrong, you would learn a lot from interviewing each person separately. But you would learn a lot more if you investigated the way they interact, the way in which the relationships between them either help each of them to work better or, alternatively, undermine their best efforts. They form a group, and how much the organization manages to do, and how well it is done, depends on the way the group works together as a group. So it is with the organs and their associated pulses. If, say, two of them seem agitated, erratic, struggling, then you need to find out both how the group as a whole is affected by that and why the group isn't able to help those two get back to normal. The state of the other ten pulses, and their relationships with the two struggling ones, should answer both of these questions: will tell you, in other words, the nature of the patient's imbalance.

Take excessive menstrual bleeding, for example. The spleen pulse is a good starting point, because the spleen governs the blood, in the sense of making sure it is in the right place at the right time. A weakness in the energy of the spleen might explain what has happened, especially if there are other indications that the spleen isn't working well – if the patient's face looks yellow and she has lost her appetite. But you would also have to look at the liver pulse too, because the liver stores blood; perhaps the excessive bleeding is partly because the liver isn't storing blood properly and menstruation is acting as a sort of overflow. Then perhaps the problem lies in the relationship between these two; maybe the spleen is all right in itself, but it is suffering knock-on effects from a problem in the liver, or vice versa. Better check the colon pulse too; perhaps it is too active, letting go too much, and the liver can't cope with that. And although kidney problems usually have the opposite effect, that is they tend to result in scanty bleeding, they are closely involved with the whole process of menstruation, so the quantity and quality of that pulse would be interesting. As you can see, there are many possibilities, and there is the whole business of disentangling which energy imbalance is a cause of the excessive bleeding, and which is a consequence of losing too much blood. But once the practitioner has learned the language of the pulses their message is clear and unequivocal.

Listening

A good practitioner of any system of medicine will know the difference between hearing and listening. At the simplest level, a good listener will take seriously what a patient is saying about his or her illness. Here is a simple story.

In the middle of a netball match, while jumping to catch a

ball, a young girl fell to the floor in pain, and when she got up she couldn't put any weight at all on her leg. She was taken to the hospital where she told the doctor that she had felt it go while she was in mid-air. The X-ray showed that she had a hairline fracture of her fibula, the smaller bone of her lower leg, and she was put in plaster for some weeks. The day the plaster came off she collapsed in pain again. So she was put back in plaster for another few weeks; clearly the fracture hadn't healed properly. When that plaster was taken off the same thing happened again. This time the registrar took over her case and talked to her about her injury. She repeated that she had felt her leg go while she was in mid-air. 'In that case,' he said thoughtfully, 'you can't have fractured it. You can't fracture your leg in mid-air. The fracture must have happened when you landed. You must have done something else as well.' He examined her more carefully and discovered that she must have dislocated her kneecap. As soon as the plaster was taken off it had dislocated again.

Of course, sometimes what the patient says isn't so clear. To be sure, he is reporting his experience of what is happening in his body as best he can, but it isn't always easy to find words for body-felt sensations, nor to describe them accurately. Still, the report is an absolutely essential clue to what is going on. I had a patient who had pain in his joints. What was odd about it was that the pain kept moving around, but was always in the arms or legs. One day, or one hour, it was in his left knee, then it moved to his left wrist and then to his right shoulder and then to his left ankle and so on, in no discernible pattern. Asked what it felt like he said 'it is as if there is a little gremlin, rushing around, attacking one joint after another.' The story of the pulses was that he had become seriously exhausted about three months before. As he had continued to work in spite of it, there just wasn't enough energy left in the system as a whole to do everything that needed doing. So essential functions, like breathing and digestion and spinal support, had been maintained and what was left over for the less important task of making the joints of the arms and legs work properly had to be severely rationed. Faced with this problem, the body, perfectly sensibly, had chosen not to give all the energy to one or two joints and leave the rest to suffer, but to make sure that none of them got too starved. So when one joint ran out of energy badly, and started to hurt, the gremlin rushed in and gave it a bit to be going on with. Then, as the next one started to complain, it rushed off there and gave it some instead, and so on. The patient's report about the gremlin was helpful, and accurate in a way; his only mistake was to assume that it was attacking when in fact it was defending.

Then there are important clues to be gained from listening to what the patient emphasizes and what he leaves out in telling his story, and even more from noticing his reactions to what the practitioner says. There are some patients who, if you offer them sympathy for having been in a lot of pain, reject it brusquely, saying 'can't complain' or 'never one to make a fuss' and change the subject as quickly as possible. Others want sympathy, some even demand sympathy, for a relatively trivial complaint, and when it is given they want more. 'Yes, my leg really did hurt, in fact it hurt so much I couldn't go on the picnic, and I was so looking forward to it because I haven't had a chance to get out for weeks I've been so busy, because I've been let down at work and I'm having to cover for Dawn and she's left things in such a mess ...' If I sympathize with these people I often feel as if I'm reaching out a hand to pull them out of a bog, and they practically pull my arm off. These extreme attitudes to sympathy speak volumes about imbalance in the energy body, specifically with the state of earth energy. They also help the practitioner to keep listening. If you see this patient as having a minor pain in his leg, then his demand for sympathy is simply tedious and aggravating. If, on the other hand, you see him as a person with an imbalance which is causing both the leg problem and the need for sympathy, then you can be as dispassionately interested in the one as the other. Also, instead of judging him, which always gets in the way of listening properly, you know that he is only craving sympathy because his energy is out of balance.

Apart from the content of what a patient says, the tone of voice in which he says it is good diagnostic information. Again, the general point is that the body gives off all sorts of signals which point clearly to the state of its energy and to any disturbance in the energy of particular organs and functions. Just as a good gardener can tell what a plant needs from the state of its leaves and flowers, so a good practitioner can tell what a body needs from its colour, its pulses, and the quality of its voice. If you listen carefully to someone you know well, you will start to notice a tone which is more or less invariant. One of the best ways of getting it is to listen to their answerphone message; that way you are not distracted by the content of the words. My sister's voice is loud, clipped and forceful. It always sounds as if she is barking out orders at a rather sloppy platoon of soldiers, or imitating the way colonial governors used to speak to their native servants. This is wood energy speaking. The forceful, sharp, outward energy of wood is perfectly communicated in the way her voice seems to be thrown at the listener. A close friend, to take another example, seems to be singing when she speaks. Her voice rises and falls, dips into softness then rises to a full-throated paean, for all the world as if she was following some half-remembered tune. By contrast to my sister's voice, it is very soothing to hear; it folds you in and wraps you up almost like a lullaby. This voice has the circular, enfolding, protecting quality of earth energy.

If it isn't easy to catch the tone of a person's voice, and some are a good deal more difficult than others, then any disparity between the content of the words and the tone of voice in which they are said will make it clear. So if someone is telling you what a wonderful holiday he had, going somewhere he'd always dreamed of visiting, but it sounds as if he's telling you about the time his computer crashed and he lost two weeks' work – if it has a sad and hopeless sighing quality to it – then you'll know that his metal energy needs attention. That is because metal energy expresses loss and grief, and if it is out of balance the tone of voice will express these things even when they are inappropriate. Normally it isn't difficult to recognize the quality of a voice; we are all very familiar with the double messages we get when its tone doesn't match the meaning of the words, and we're especially good at grasping what our loved ones are telling us, behind the words. Depending on the tone of voice used, saying 'if you really want to do that, I'll help' can mean 'I know it is difficult for you but I'm behind you all the way' or 'you must be crazy, but I suppose if I don't help it'll be a complete disaster, so I'll have to.' To use this everyday skill diagnostically, you have only to learn to match the particular tones of voice with particular energy states.

Smell

Using smell for diagnosis is as old as the hills. Army and navy surgeons have used it for centuries to tell if there is gangrene in a wound, and most mothers know if their child is ill because of a change in his or her normal odour. What was well known in traditional medicine, but has been largely forgotten, is that a patient has a normal or background odour, and the way it changes gives highly specific information about what is going on inside the body. My normal odour is a kind of slightly burnt smell, like hot sand or a newly ironed shirt; when I had pneumonia this took on an extra acrid quality. The overall result was a rather distasteful hot rotting smell, like a compost heap which has got too wet or a rubbish tip in a hot country (maybe, like me, you've never actually smelled a rubbish tip in a hot country, but you get the idea). Another smell I know well is a slightly sour one, like milk that has been left out in the sun and is about to go off.

It can be difficult to catch these odours, partly because there is such a taboo about body odour. Most people pretend they don't have one, while at the same time they use perfumes of one kind or another to conceal it. We all pretend that others don't have one either. And there is a real difficulty too, because our noses get used to smells very quickly. With faint odours, we only have a few seconds to pick them up. If you are interested, pay real attention to the odour when you first walk into a room where someone has been on his or her own for a while; that first, immediate impression is often clear. So too when someone takes off the clothes he or she has been wearing all day.

The sixth sense

I think we use this sense a lot more often than we realize, especially when we are using the knowledge gained through many years of experience. I was in a restaurant once with a married couple who own a restaurant themselves. As a party of four walked in, the husband of the couple glanced up at them and then said to his wife 'they'll send the food back'; she nodded as if it was the most obvious thing in the world. And indeed they did (enraging the chef to such an extent that he appeared in the dining room brandishing half a lamb carcass). I asked them how they knew, but they had no idea; they just knew. Practitioners do this too: 'an elderly Chinese doctor with whom I once studied… watched a stranger enter a room and promptly asked him when he'd had his gall bladder removed.'

Most of the time there is nothing remarkable about this at all. When the husband glanced up he was collecting a vast amount of information and then comparing it with information he had gathered from a huge number of similar situations in the past: as there was a good fit between the two, he drew the obvious conclusion that the outcome would be the same this time as it was before. It seems mysterious simply because he wasn't aware of this process; it happened automatically, unconsciously, instinctively. So when a practitioner has seen many, many patients, has worked with them over the years, has an enormous mental library of their conditions, and knows the outcome of their treatments, he or she develops this sixth sense. I imagine that the elderly Chinese doctor was simply aware that the energy of the gall bladder was missing in the stranger who entered a room. If he wanted to talk about what he did, in that moment, and wanted to teach others to do it too, then he would probably be able to analyze his impressions and say something about the patient's body shape, his posture, the colour on his face and so on. That would be true enough as far as it goes, but breaking the diagnostic signs down into different categories may miss another truth, which is that the process of 'just knowing' is one of synthesis. It is putting together a host of impressions and finding that there is only one possible explanation for them all.

All this applies to any system of medicine, but there are some specific aspects of this kind of sixth sense that apply to energy medicine. One of them is the effect of the client's energy on the practitioner or on the atmosphere in the room. If suddenly, and for no apparent reason, I find myself feeling slightly hostile towards a patient, it is quite likely that I am being affected by his energy of anger or frustration. So too if I find myself going very quiet and still, as if there is something very delicate happening which mustn't be disturbed, I am probably picking up the patient's grief. What is going on is that the patient's energy body is extending outwards and overlapping with that of the practitioner. This happens partly because there is a natural tendency to fall in to the energy state of anyone you're with, and partly because another person's strong energy can be overwhelming. If the practitioner is aware of what is happening to his own energy he knows, as if by a sixth sense, what is happening to his patient's.

Similarly, in the course of a session it is quite normal to feel a change in the atmosphere in the room. This can be delightful, like the sun coming out after a day of greyness and drizzling rain, or the kind of quietness you feel when you walk into an old forest. On the other hand, it can be alarming, like the tension in the air when people are being ultra-polite with each other to avoid saying the unforgivable things they are dying to say. Whichever it is, it speaks of a change in the patient's energy, and as soon as the practitioner understands why it changed just then and why it changed in that way, he is well on the way to knowing how to help.

Apart from all this, there are some people who have what I would call a genuine sixth sense; that is they can diagnose in ways which are a real mystery. Caroline Myss is a so-called medical intuitive who has worked extensively with a very well-known American neurosurgeon. Normally, the patient is sitting in the neurosurgeon's office while he telephones Caroline, telling her only the patient's name and date of birth. She then reports what is wrong with the patient. Over many trials, she has been found to be accurate in 93% of cases, a quite extraordinary accomplishment. What is especially interesting and relevant here is that she says she gets her information from the state of the patient's energy, even over the telephone.

> As I sense the quality of energy throughout a person's body, I look for 'hot spots' or areas where the vibration is noticeably different than it should be normally. These hot spots indicate the presence of bodily dysfunction and the exact nature of the illness.

> Caroline Myss and C. Norman Shealy

And she says that the way she does this is by paying very deliberate and very close attention to changes in her own energy.

Attention

I said earlier that the process of diagnosis can be therapeutic in itself. When a practitioner is paying real attention to his patient, which he has to do in order to perceive the state of his or her energy body and the messages it is communicating, that attention has a powerful effect. If you are talking about something which matters to you and someone really listens, concentrating hard not on trying to think of what he will say next nor on finding the holes in your argument or on trying to remember what you said the last time you talked, but on what you are actually trying to say now and what you want understood, even though you can't always find the right words for it, it is like soothing lotion on sunburnt skin. When people talk about their illness and the effect it is having on their lives and those of their families, they are talking about something which is vitally important to them and also difficult to explain. If they feel heard and understood, if they feel that the practitioner has recognized in some way the pain, the embarrassments, the difficulties of that illness, that makes a difference. The same is true if someone really looks at you, and instead of their eyes slipping past, they notice how you are feeling, and notice too what troubles you and what brings you ease. The same is true if someone touches you not casually nor in a practical, efficient sort of way, but with a real sensitivity to how you want to be touched and with an inquiring desire to learn more about you – and to learn only as much as you are willing to reveal and at your own pace.

All this evokes a change in the patient. Obviously we could simply say that he or she will relax, feel more at ease and so on. But that's a bit like saying that someone who has just fallen passionately in love is feeling happy. It doesn't begin to describe the power of the experience nor the dramatic effects it can have. A person who falls in love like that can abandon long-held beliefs in a moment, can venture into enormous life changes without a second thought, and can find that chronic complaints just disappear. The relationship between a patient and a practitioner who is paying real attention to him or her has quite a lot in common with falling in love. The close attention creates an unmistakable intimacy, something deep which is hard to talk about has been touched and there is a distinct change in the energy body which will, sooner or later, change the physical body.

There are countless stories which demonstrate this. Here is one which I find particularly eloquent and inspiring and which also encapsulates much of the content of this chapter. It was written by a doctor at a prestigious medical school.

> On the bulletin board in the front hall of the hospital where I work there appeared an announcement. 'Yeshi Dhonden,' it read, 'will make rounds at six o'clock in the morning of June 10.' The particulars were then given, followed by a notation: 'Yeshi Dhonden is personal physician to the Dalai Lama.'

> … on the morning of June 10, I join a clutch of whitecoats waiting in the small conference room adjacent to the ward selected for the rounds. The air in the room is heavy with ill-concealed dubiety and suspicion of bamboozlement. At precisely six o' clock he materializes, a short, golden, barrelly man dressed in a sleeveless robe of saffron and maroon. His scalp is shaven and the only visible hair is a scanty black line above each hooded eye.

> He bows in greeting while his young interpreter makes the introduction. Yeshi Dhonden, we are told, will examine a patient selected by a member of the staff. The diagnosis is unknown to Yeshi Dhonden, as it is to us …

The patient had been awakened early and told that she was to be examined by a foreign doctor, and had been asked to produce a fresh specimen of urine, so when we enter her room the woman shows no surprise. She has long ago taken on that mixture of compliance and resignation that is the face of chronic illness. This was to be but another in an endless series of tests and examinations. Yeshi Dhonden steps to the bedside while the rest of us stand apart, watching. For a long time he gazes at the woman, favoring no part of her body with his eyes, but seeming to fix his glance at a place just above her supine form. I, too, study her. No physical sign or obvious symptom gives a clue to the nature of her disease.

At last he takes her hand, raising it in both of his own. Now he bends over the bed in a kind of crouching stance, his head drawn down into the collar of his robe. His eyes are closed as he feels for her pulse. In a moment he has found the spot, and for the next half-hour he remains thus, suspended over the patient like some exotic golden bird with folded wings, holding the pulse of the woman beneath his fingers, cradling her hand in his. All the power of the man seems to have been drawn down into this one purpose. It is palpation of the pulse raised to the state of ritual. From the foot of the bed, where I stand, it is as though he and the patient have entered a special place of isolation, of apartness, about which a vacancy hovers, and across which no violation is possible. After a moment the woman rests back upon her pillow. From time to time she raises her head to look at the strange figure above her, then sinks back once more. I can see their hands joined in a correspondence that is exclusive, intimate, his fingertips receiving the voice of her sick body through the rhythm and throb she offers at her wrist. All at once I am envious – not of him … but of her. I want to be held like that, touched so, received. And I know that I, who have palpated a hundred thousand pulses, have not felt a single one.

At last Yeshi Dhonden straightens, gently places the woman's hand upon the bed, and steps back. The interpreter produces a small wooden bowl and two sticks. Yeshi Dhonden pours a portion of the urine specimen into the bowl and proceeds to whip the liquid with two sticks. This he does for several minutes until a foam is raised. Then, bowing over the bowl, he inhales the odour three times. He sets down the bowl and turns to leave. All this while he has not uttered a single word.

As her nears the door, the woman raises her head and calls to him in a voice at once urgent and serene. 'Thank you, doctor,' she says, and touches with her other hand the place he had held on her wrist, as through to recapture something that had visited there …

We are seated once more in the conference room. Yeshi Dhonden speaks now for the first time in soft Tibetan sounds that I have never heard before. He has barely begun when the young interpreter begins to translate … Between the chambers of the heart, long, long before she was born, a wind had come and blown open a deep gate that must never be opened. Through it charge the full waters of her river, as the mountain stream cascades in the springtime, battering, knocking

*loose the land, and flooding her breath. Thus he
speaks and now is silent.*

'May we now have the diagnosis?' a professor asks.

*The host of the rounds, the man who knows,
answers. 'Congenital heart disease,' he says.
'Interventricular septal defect, with resultant
heart failure.'*

*A gateway in the heart, I think. That must not be
opened. Through it charge the full waters that flood
her breath. So! Here then is the doctor listening to the
sounds of the body to which the rest of us are deaf.*

Ram Dass and Paul Gorman

Chapter 5

The therapeutic relationship

When I asked Dr Schweitzer how he accounted for the fact that anyone could possibly expect to become well after having been treated by a witch doctor, he said I was asking him to divulge a secret that doctors have carried around with them ever since Hippocrates.

'But I'll tell you anyway,' he said, his face still illuminated by that half smile. 'The witch doctor succeeds for the same reason all the rest of us succeed. Each patient carries his own doctor inside him. They come to us not knowing that truth. We are at our best when we give the doctor who resides within each patient a chance to go to work.'

Norman Cousins

When I was a child I was ill a lot. When I didn't feel well enough to go to school, the doctor would be summoned to examine me. I can still remember the tension of it, like waiting for a jury to proclaim guilt or innocence. If the decision went one way, I would stay at home and be cosseted: if it went the other, I would be bunged out on my ear and made to go into school late, which was awkward and embarrassing, especially as I would have hanging over me all day, like a mist on a mountain top, the faint but distinct air of fraudulence. It all turned on a name. If the doctor, unlooping his stethoscope, were to say to my mother 'it's bronchitis,' then I'd be all right.

If you look up bronchitis in a medical dictionary you'll find it means an inflammation of the tubes between the lungs and the mouth and nose. If you look up inflammation, you'll find it means redness, swelling, heat, and sometimes pain, in tissue. So the magic word which got me off school meant that I had red, swollen, hot tissue in those tubes. It didn't explain much; it didn't tell me what had caused it nor what to do to make sure I didn't get it again. It didn't tell me whether it would be better to go to school or better to stay in bed. It did mean that I was given some unpleasant medicine to take, but no one really knew if that was what made me better, or made me better more quickly. It may seem as if it was a pointless exercise, but that is to ignore the ritual of it all. The ritual was to do with warding off danger. There was danger in the house. I might be sickening for something serious. On the other hand, I might be trying to skive off because I hadn't done my homework; to allow me not to go to school would be to court the lesser danger that I would learn to bluff and to get away with things. The ritual dispelled the danger in such a way that everyone was satisfied. My feeling of being ill was legitimated. My mother was affirmed and comforted at the same time – she was told that it was worth worrying, but not to get too worried – because the doctor knew what it was, it was under control. The doctor's importance to his patients and status in the community had been enhanced. And the National Health Service paid for it all.

It is extraordinarily powerful, this ritual of naming an illness. It does so many things at once. For a start, it says that you aren't imagining what you are feeling, you aren't just making a fuss about nothing, you aren't a hypochondriac nor do you have a laughably low pain threshold. Someone in authority has confirmed that it is reasonable and legitimate to feel what you are feeling. Next, once your illness is named you are relieved from practically all the obligations you have in normal life. You don't have to go to school or work, cook, pick up the children, make conversation, or even be interested in anyone else; and if you do any of these things in spite of being ill you are regarded as heroic and noble. Others do things for you and at the same time you are entitled to a good deal of sympathy. It is a state which certainly has its attractions, especially if there are jobs you don't want to do or meetings you don't want to attend, and a medical diagnosis is the passport to that state. People go to the doctor to get that passport, and the doctor makes sure that it isn't given to an illegal immigrant – someone who is not entitled to enter the state of illness.

Behind all this is the rather odd belief that you aren't really ill unless the doctor says so. Whether or not you are ill cannot actually depend on what someone else thinks; how it feels is all that matters and it can't be fully known by anyone else. But doctors and patients collude in maintaining this fiction. The patient wants the technical diagnostic term which is an official and public statement that 'he can't do this, that or the other, and it isn't his fault'. The doctor needs to make a diagnosis of a recognized and understood illness because only then can she prescribe a treatment which is accepted as appropriate according to her professional training. In other words, the fiction is useful. It keeps the system working and no doubt helps quite a lot of patients. And it creates a very particular kind of relationship between doctor and patient. Energy medicine, which doesn't diagnose illness but imbalance, creates a different kind of relationship between practitioner and patient.

Tests and objectivity

Routinely, a doctor will take samples of tissue or body fluids and send them off for analysis. No diagnosis, or at any rate no firm diagnosis, can be made until the report has come back. If it shows some deviation from a norm, for example if the number of blood cells is abnormally high or abnormally low, then the doctor can prescribe a treatment based on that diagnosis. Similarly, the doctor may order X-rays or an MRI scan of the body to find out what is going on inside, unseen. This is all perfectly sensible and straightforward, but it has changed one aspect of diagnosis. What was traditionally the outcome of an intimate personal interaction between doctor and patient is now carried out in the laboratory – far from the patient and in terms which mean nothing to him or her. The process of diagnosis happens less in the consulting room and more in the laboratory.

What is lost is the kind of close attention paid by the doctor to the patient which I described in the last chapter. This kind of attention has its own powerful therapeutic effect. This is well known in the world of organizational consultancy, where it is called 'the Hawthorne effect' after the name of the factory where it was first formally identified.

In the 1930s researchers went into an organization to study how particular tasks were done by a group of workers; the idea was that after they'd watched them for a while, the researchers would be able to suggest all sorts of ways of improving productivity. What they discovered was that while they were there, watching, productivity soared. Investigating this phenomenon, they discovered it wasn't because the workers were pulling up their socks, nervous of what the researchers might report; it was because they felt that if the managers thought it was worth getting researchers in to study them they must be important to the organization. They also felt that, having been observed so closely over quite a long period of time, the researchers understood them and their jobs and the difficulties they faced. As a result they felt proud, motivated and keen to display their full potential. The researchers then discovered that this held good whatever organization they studied; just their presence, watching carefully, boosted productivity irrespective of any expertise they might have or any recommendations they might make – intelligent or otherwise. Many organizational consultants have made a good living out of the Hawthorne effect ever since.

Just as we all know how awful it feels when someone ignores us, or ignores what matters deeply to us, we know how supportive and satisfying it feels when someone pays real attention to us. Of course, we are quite choosy about it. Some people like attention which takes the form of close questioning and a persistent direct look. Others, who would find that intrusive and embarrassing, want a softer, more tactful approach. The point is that if the patient gets real attention, in much the same way as the Hawthorne work group got real attention, that will mobilize his or her potential, in this case potential for healing. Here are two examples of how it works.

In traditional trials of new drugs, some patients are given the drug and others are given sugared water or some other substance which has no known benefits: it's called a placebo. What is well known is that a significant proportion of the patients given the placebo do better than expected. This is normally explained as follows – if a patient believes he or she is taking a drug which will help, then that belief is a self-fulfilling prophecy. It is mind over matter again. To check that the drug being tested is more effective than just taking sugared water, the trials make statistical allowance for this placebo effect. In other words, in the search for new cures, peoples' gullibility is a bit of a nuisance and has to be discounted. But one study turned this idea on its head. It argued that it would be an immense boon if people could get better from taking sugared water. It would save a fortune on drugs and would avoid all the problems of side effects from, and addiction to, prescribed drugs. In what circumstances, it asked, could the placebo effect be amplified and enhanced? What would make it work better?

The study came up with a number of factors which could increase the effectiveness of placebos, but most of them were about the quality of the relationship between the practitioner and the patient. So, for example, the placebo was more effective if the patient felt the practitioner really understood what it was like to be ill in the particular way that he or she was ill: and the patient only felt that when the practitioner gave real attention to the patient's story. Another key factor was the creation of a shared understanding of the nature of the illness, of how to tackle it, and of what the patient could do to help himself heal. Clearly, if the diagnosis is only in technical scientific language, there won't be any real shared understanding.

For example, I recently treated a young woman who was complaining of very itchy eyes. Although it was in early June, the classic time for hay fever, she didn't think it was that. I asked her if she had any other symptoms, because it really helps to pin down the nature of the imbalance if there are two or more symptoms, but she said 'no'. When I took her pulses the small intestine seemed to be fine – as I mentioned in Chapter 3, this organ and this function is normally under stress if pollen is a problem. But it was clear to me that her earth energy, and particularly that of the stomach, was very weak, depleted, struggling. That was suggestive, because the stomach meridian starts just below the eye. I asked her if she'd had trouble eating; 'Oh yes,' she said. 'I started a new slimming diet two weeks ago and I was supposed to take some pills with it. I did it for a day or two, then I was away on business and I couldn't stick to the diet – in fact I hardly had time to eat at all, but I kept on taking the pills. Then, when I got back, I started the diet again but stupidly I kept forgetting to take the pills. Then I felt sick when I ate.' So I told her that I thought that this was what had made her eyes dry up, explaining about the energy of the stomach and where it flows. She was fascinated. I said that given this imbalance, I would have expected her to have been constipated too; she said she had been. I gave her a treatment to boost her earth energy, but most of the treatment was really in the diagnosis. Now she understood what had happened and why, she also knew how to deal with the problem of itchy eyes if it recurred.

The overall point is that devoting time and attention to patients, really gaining an understanding of them and their complaints, talking it over with them in terms they can understand, really helps people to get better – whether they are taking expensive drugs, homeopathic remedies or coloured water, having surgery, chiropractice or acupuncture. When effort is put into building up this kind of relationship, the apparently clear dividing line between diagnosis and treatment disappears. The diagnosis is a key part of the treatment and the dialogue with the patient has a marked therapeutic effect. This is lost when diagnosis is carried out by a different person in a different place.

Collaboration in wellness

If a patient has a back pain and a slipped disc, it is easy to make a diagnosis that the slipped disc is causing the pain. But it may not be true.

> The speaker ... gave a fascinating lecture on the lack of correlation between the subjective experience of back pain and objective measures of musculoskeletal dysfunction, such as X-rays and MRI scans. He showed X-rays and scans of patients that looked so

awful you could not believe these people could stand
or walk, yet they were free from pain and had normal
mobility. In other cases, people were immobilized by
pain, yet their spines looked normal.

Andrew Weil

It may be that something else is causing both the slipped disc
and the pain, independently, so to speak. Or it may be that the
disc isn't the ultimate cause, just part of the knock-on effects of
some other, older cause. If, for example, the patient broke a
bone in his left foot and, while recovering from that injury, got
into the habit of walking with most of his weight on his right
foot, that would put an uneven strain on his right hip, his
sacroiliac joint, and his lumbar spine. His back, including the
disc, would be affected in all sorts of ways. If he can learn to
walk with his weight evenly distributed on both legs, then the
disc may slip back into place; or his back pain may cease even
if the disc remains out of place. There are many possibilities
without even beginning to consider the relevance of what else
is going on in the patient's life: long habits of working at
a computer which is at a desk off to one side of his chair,
financial worries, strains in his marriage and so on.

    If any of these are relevant, then the patient will have to
be recruited into the whole process of treatment; and in order
to do that he or she will have to be recruited into understanding and appreciating the diagnosis.

A guy gets his back or his hip or something out of
order and goes to a manipulator who adjusts it. He
says 'Oh, that's wonderful,' but he goes down the
stairs and by the time he's on the street it's back again.
He hadn't learned a different organization.
Organization is dynamic. Organization in the body is
not static; it is the way muscles are used in

> *movement. In order to make a significant difference*
> *... the man's whole system has to be taught a new,*
> *more balanced, organization.*

> Ida Rolf

This point holds good for more than just pain, more than just manipulation. Orange juice aggravates arthritis. The best treatment in the world won't work if the patient insists on continuing to drink gallons of the stuff. If someone's hair is falling out because she is working too hard (according to energy medicine exhaustion particularly affects the kidneys, and the kidneys generate the growth of hair on the head) then no amount of treatment will reverse the hair loss until she cuts back on her workload. The time with a practitioner is only a tiny part of the patient's life; sooner or later he or she must learn to live in a way that will maintain and amplify the effects of the treatment during the days and weeks between sessions. The treatment and the patient's way of life have to be consistent, to be mutually reinforcing, in order to bring about change. And it is the practitioner's job to instigate a mutual search for that consistency, to start to find out how the patient can best collaborate in the process of change. It is no use ordering an elderly patient to lose weight, however much it may help him to do so, if his only remaining pleasure in life is eating good food and drinking good wine. If he won't do it – it might be fairer to say 'given that he can't do it' – nothing will have been achieved except to make him feel guilty every time he does the only thing he enjoys. It would be just as bad telling someone with a serious liver complaint, and who is eager to get better, that a few drinks here and there won't matter; they will. These are obvious examples: in most situations it is quite a complex business to negotiate exactly what changes the patient can make which are both feasible and desirable – and, as with all negotiations, the way it is conducted can make all the difference to the outcome.

If the process of diagnosis is seen less as a search for a thing, like a microbe, a hormone deficiency, or a slipped disc, and more as a search for the way in which the patient and the practitioner can best work together, then what matters is not so much the cause of the illness but the creation, the maintenance and the deepening of the relationship between the two of them. It isn't surprising that this should be so important. At times of illness patients are anxious, perhaps terrified, fragile and vulnerable. One thing they need badly is someone who knows them well, who takes a real interest in them and their illness (relatives and friends, with the best will in the world, tend to get bored), who will stick with them through thick and thin, and who will share an expertise, whatever it is.

I've mentioned that a large part of this collaboration is a search for a common understanding of the illness. If the practitioner believes she knows what is wrong, but the patient doesn't accept or doesn't understand the diagnosis, then they can't collaborate. Of course, any system of medicine will have its technical terms, its categorizations which mean nothing to someone who hasn't had the training. What I am getting at is that the practitioner must be able to talk about what might be going on in such a way that the two of them can arrive at a shared view of the meaning of the illness. Once the woman with itchy eyes understood the connection between her eyes and her stomach, then she knew that as soon as her eyes started to dry up she had to pay more attention to her diet. The practitioner, for his part, will know that he isn't being expected to fix the problem – an expectation which may lead him to attempt quick and dramatic cures, which may offer temporary relief or may fail entirely – but can work steadily to enhance the patient's own healing, using whatever technique he practises. And they will each play their part more effectively because they will be sharing information about the progress of the treatment in terms which they both understand. If her eyes start up again, she will know that the chances are she is falling back into old habits, rather than assuming that the treatment hasn't worked: and he will know that he can help her stomach to be more robust without being expected to make her eyes better on demand.

Generalizing from this example, the practitioner has two things to offer. One is the particular skill or technique in which she is trained. The other is a sensitive and accurate assessment, both of each patient's capacity for change and of the way in which it can best be stimulated. This is different for every patient. Some of them will be receptive to whatever they can do to help, will be willing to look at all aspects of their life to see what might make a difference, and confident that they can be well again. They may only need a little encouragement and a helping hand. Others will be feeling hopeless and resigned, inured to pain and discomfort and not really expecting it to get better. They may need a more interventionist approach at first, to feel that something is being done, and then a very gradual and patient coaching to teach them how they can help themselves. Some patients will be physically weak; others will be robust in spite of their illness. Some may find emotional pain unbearable, and will do practically anything, including being ill, to avoid it. The variety is endless. The practitioner's job is to find how best to help each patient set in motion his own self-healing, to 'give the doctor who resides within each patient a chance to go to work'.

Sooner or later, and usually sooner, this involves a search for the patient's underlying wellness. Inside each patient, and not quite forgotten however ill he may be, is a part of him which is perfectly well. It is one of those shifts of perception. You experience it with the picture which seems to be of a black vase; if you look at it again, your perception can suddenly change and you can see it as two white faces in profile, looking at each other (Figure 11).

It's a bit the same with illness. The patient starts by seeing

Figure 11

illness; otherwise she wouldn't have come for treatment at all. It is the practitioner's task also to see the wellness, and then to help the patient see it too. More than see it actually – experience it, know it, and foster it. This is critically important. If the patient only sees illness, she sees an enemy which must be defeated, and that brings in its wake a host of attitudes and expectations which can get in the way of healing. For one thing, it fosters a very aggressive attitude to the body, when all it is doing is trying to communicate a message of distress and to indicate the path back to health. Hitting the messenger on the head to make it shut up doesn't help. In fact, it probably means that the messenger will shout louder, by creating a more serious complaint or a more severe pain, in order to get the patient to listen. If, on the other hand, the patient can be helped to focus on his underlying wellness, then it becomes natural to pay close attention to the meaning of symptoms, to start to think about how the body can be helped, supported, encouraged rather than fought; how all its forces, again mental and emotional as well as physical, can be united to amplify its underlying wellness and capacity for healing. Thinking about what makes you well has a very different effect from thinking about what makes you ill.

Dr Oliver Sacks, the well-known neurologist, knows this perfectly well. In the case of Dr P., a classical singer, he managed to see past his patient's baffling degenerative disease to the part of him that was brilliantly well.

> A few days later I called on Dr P. and his wife at home ... Dr P. came in, a little bowed, and, distracted, advanced with outstretched hand to the grandfather clock, but, hearing my voice, corrected himself and shook hands with me. We exchanged greetings and chatted a little of current concerts and performances. Diffidently, I asked him if he would sing.
>
> 'The Dichterliebe' he exclaimed. 'But I can no longer read music. You will play them, yes?'
>
> I said I would try. On that wonderful old piano even my playing sounded right, and Dr P. was an aged but infinitely mellow Fischer-Dieskau, combining a perfect ear and voice with the most incisive musical intelligence ...
>
> 'Well, Dr Sacks,' he said to me, 'You find me an interesting case, I perceive. Can you tell me what you find wrong, make recommendations?'
>
> 'I can't tell you what I find wrong,' I replied, 'but I'll say what I find right. You are a wonderful musician, and music is your life. What I would prescribe, in a case such as yours, is a life which consists entirely of music ...'

Oliver Sacks

It is difficult to write eloquently enough about this. Focusing on wellness instead of illness, everything looks different. It's like looking at a view through one end of a telescope, and then turning it round and seeing the view through the other end. When you look for what's wrong, it is so easy to develop tunnel vision; both the doctor and the patient are led, almost inexorably, into an ever more detailed examination of the minute, the one critical thing that will make all the difference. It leads to doctors identifying illness exclusively with microbes, and unconsciously assuming that nothing else really matters. It leads patients to become obsessive about the minutiae of their medication – is this pill the right one? Did I take two yesterday or three? Should I search the Internet for a new treatment which my doctor hasn't heard of? Dare I go on holiday, far from anyone who knows about my case? Where is the nearest hospital? The patient becomes an 'interesting case', both to himself and to his doctor: that is, someone who must be investigated over and over again in ever more recondite ways for the breakthrough, the new medical knowledge that will save the day. That depersonalizes the process, and suggests that the way this individual is living his life is irrelevant. The more that an illness is investigated in this way, the more it takes on a kind of life of its own; it is being studied as a natural phenomenon, rather as a zoologist might study a population of beetles, and both patient and doctor become fascinated by it. It may seem an exaggeration, but if the illness were to suddenly go away, for no apparent reason, then as well as being pleased they might both feel slightly cheated, as if they had lost something.

A search for wellness leads both patient and practitioner down a very different path. One key question which they will address is how the patient can do more of the things that bring him joy and satisfaction. It may be that the activities which used to give him these pleasures are no longer available; his illness makes them impossible. It is vital, then, to find alternatives.

*Hans Sayle ... showed that adrenal exhaustion could
be caused by emotional tension, such as frustration or
suppressed rage. He detailed the negative effects of the
negative emotions on body chemistry. The inevitable
question arose in my mind; what about the positive
emotions? If negative emotions produce negative
chemical changes in the body, wouldn't the positive
emotions produce positive chemical changes? Is it
possible that love, hope, faith, laughter, confidence,
and the will to live have therapeutic value?*

Norman Cousins

With a little ingenuity, and making full allowances for any
physical disability, the practitioner and the patient may be able
to think of all sorts of things he can do which will bring him
'love, hope, faith, laughter'. This is something that a patient's
friends and family can get involved in too, and that has untold
benefits. A person who is seriously ill can't help feeling a sense
of isolation from his family who, with the best will in the world,
don't really understand what it is like to be him. And the family
can feel isolated too; they have to live in an atmosphere of
apprehension and tension, they feel frustrated and powerless,
they have all the problems of looking after an invalid and they
may find it hard to talk to him about it. Collaborating on activities which will help the patient recover a sense of joy and
purpose in life can reunite the family and that in itself will help
the healing. The whole family joins in a diagnosis of wellness.

Then the obvious question is no longer 'what is making
this person ill?' but 'what is stopping this person getting better?'
Given that the body has a most remarkable and extraordinarily efficient self-healing system – think of how well it works
when you cut yourself or break a bone – then the enlightening
question is, 'why isn't that system operating now, or not operating well enough to sort out the problem?' This question

opens a whole new territory to explore. Answers might be found in anything from poor diet to long forgotten trauma, from recent grief to lack of exercise, from anxiety about aging to too much time spent in aeroplanes. Or, more likely, some combination of factors. If you place too many demands on the body, and dealing with emotional or spiritual distress is a major demand just as much as surviving on a poor diet, it won't be able to work properly. If it can't do everything then, perfectly sensibly, it stops doing the least urgent things first. So it will use its resources to maintain breathing, the heart beat, body temperature and so on. Loss of the self-healing system isn't life threatening – at least for a long time – so it comes low on the list of priorities. At times of stress, that system is starved of resources quite quickly. It sounds so banal and trite to say that if you are ill then look to reduce what is causing you stress. It sounds less banal if it is presented, completely realistically, as a way of altering blood pressure, relieving back pain, or altering the alkaline phosphotase enzyme count in the liver from 400 to 150.

The search for wellness isn't only relevant when people are ill; it is just as important when they have no obvious or troublesome symptom. Prevention is always better than cure; knowing what keeps you well, and ensuring that you have enough of it, means that you are much less likely to get ill and that you will recover much more quickly if you do succumb. But there is more to it than that. Having an energy medicine treatment simply to feel really well may sound a bit silly, a rather pampering and self-indulgent luxury, but I think that is to belittle something wonderful.

> In our culture we focus so much on illness and disease that we undervalue being genuinely well. We think of therapy of all kinds as the removal of what we don't want, rather than the fostering and enhancement of what we do. But the ability to live life to the full, to have

*the capacity to respond vigorously to a joyful occasion –
or even to a sad and painful one – is a great gift. With
that ability goes the confidence and clarity to make good
choices in life: those that will lead a person to make the
best use of their talents and realize their dreams.
Creativity flourishes, fear loses some of its grip and the
burdens of the past can be put down more easily. With
this come benefits for others too. Someone in this state is
a joy to be with and, when called upon to help, is more
present for the person in need.*

John Hamwee

Simply not being ill is too low an expectation. Diagnosis should have higher expectations and bigger ambitions.

Refinement and progress

From the start of the diagnosis everything starts to change – the relationship between patient and practitioner, the depth of their collaboration, the emergence of the patient's inner wellness, the course of the illness, the patient's attitude to that illness, the state of his energy body and so on. So, as treatment progresses, the practitioner will have to make a fresh diagnosis at each session in order to find what will best help, given the current state of all these aspects of the joint undertaking. If progress is slow, the diagnosis at the fifth treatment may be pretty much the same as it was at the first, but there will be some refinement as the practitioner learns more about the patient and his energy body, and can see, with more accuracy and sophistication, what might help. More often change gets underway quite quickly and new diagnoses are needed regularly. Like most practitioners I've been caught out by this. I've given a treatment which worked especially well; impressed and delighted at the results, I've repeated it a few weeks later only to find that it did nothing. The patient has moved on since the last time.

This is another aspect of getting to know 'the patient who has the disease' rather than 'the disease that has the patient'. As each person falls ill in an individual way, so each person gets better in an individual way. I have watched great practitioners of energy medicine who, at the first meeting with a patient, seem to be able to predict a great deal about that person's path back to health. They can see, somehow, the way that a person's energy will change – given its character and its current state. As C. G. Jung said, in a different context, 'What happens to a person is characteristic of him. He represents a pattern and all the pieces fit' – including, presumably, how he or she will get well. But whatever the practitioner's level of skill and insight, the future is not perfectly predictable, and the most accurate and effective treatments will be based on a fresh assessment of the client at each session.

The point is that energy changes fast. Just before I sat down to write this, I had a phone call from a friend who knows nothing about energy medicine. She told me that she'd had some people to stay for the weekend. She said she enjoyed having them, but they had left her drained. I asked her if she had been doing too much cooking, cleaning and showing them round the countryside in which she lives. 'No,' she replied, 'it's just the effect they had on me.' We have all noticed this; within the course of a day, even an hour or two, our energy levels can drop with disappointment or rise with elation. Multiply that kind of experience over weeks or months or years of an illness, and you can see that the nature of the process by which you receive medical help is critical for your prospects of recovery. If it drains your energy – waiting for appointments, for test results, having to explain your symptoms over and over again to different people, trying many different drugs to find the one which is going to suddenly work like magic, having your hopes lifted by one that seems at first to work but then being frustrated when its effect tails off – then you simply have less energy to fuel your healing. If, on the other hand, the process is instructive, interesting, involving; if you feel that someone is walking the path with you and supporting you through the difficulties; if reverses can be seen as a stimulus to a fresh or deeper understanding of yourself; then all that will boost your energy and, hopefully, give you enough to get your own healing system working well again.

Certainly, cells and tissue and bones change more slowly than energy, and they have to heal too; the results of a quick change in the energy body may not register in the physical body for some time. But, to quote Valerie Hunt again: 'Electromedical researchers believe that each disease or functional disturbance has its own energy field which must be reversed before healing can take place.' The first meeting between patient and practitioner is an opportunity to make a start on reversing that energy field, because it will be affected by the energy field of the practitioner and, more important, by the energy field of the relationship itself. The better the relationship, over the weeks and months of treatment, the better the diagnosis and the better the effects of treatment. Not for some vague reason, but specifically and reliably, because the energy of the relationship is part of the diagnosis and part of the treatment. All three together amplify the process of change.

Chapter 6

How treatment works

Therapeutic interventions don't cause anything. They resonate with the possibility that was always there.

Ted Kaptchuk

If you listen to music you love, especially if it is played loudly, it evokes strong sensations. They aren't quite emotions, but you feel them powerfully and physically. Some of the mysterious power of music comes from the fact that the vibrations of the instruments – strings, wind instruments, drums – and of the singing voice enter the body and have a direct physical effect. The sound resonates in your chest rather as the sound of a vibrating violin string resonates inside the body of the violin. But it isn't just the air in your chest which is affected, so are the lungs and the heart. These organs are flexible living tissue and, rather like blancmanges on top of a washing machine, they vibrate in response to the vibration of the music. So too do ribs, although you'd need very sensitive instruments to pick that up.

Because we are normally unaware of our bones and organs we assume that they are static, solid and unchanging; in fact they are all in a constant process of repair and renewal and they are all vibrating the whole time. Under normal conditions each organ has its own typical vibration. That's just another way of saying that each of the organs has its own kind of energy, but I want to use the term vibration in this chapter because a good deal is known about vibrations, and in particular what happens when two or more vibrations meet. With loud music, the waves or vibrations of sound sweep through the body and as they meet the existing vibrations of the organs and bones, they change them. The strong sensation you can feel in your chest comes from this change of vibration in the body. This is at least part of the reason why music can soothe, comfort and console you on the one hand, or aggravate, disturb and annoy you on the other. If the vibrations of the music meet your own inner vibrations harmoniously you'll feel better: if they clash with them, you'll feel worse.

Energy medicine treatments work in the same way. The treatment provides new vibrations which, when they come into contact with the existing vibrations in the body, change them.

If the idea of vibrations sounds a bit feeble, too weak to change anything, think of the famous Tacoma Valley Bridge disaster in America. A long suspension bridge, which had carried traffic for many years, started to vibrate gently in a crosswind. As the wind increased in strength, so did the vibrations. Eventually they got so huge that cars were flung off the road, the supporting cables started to twang like Jimmy Hendrix's guitar strings, and finally the bridge shattered and collapsed. Since then engineers have found ways of preventing this happening, at least when it's windy. However, when people flocked to walk across London's millennium footbridge between St Paul's Cathedral and the Tate Modern art gallery it started to sway, and quite quickly the swaying became so strong that people were clutching at the handrails and staggering to the end feeling sick. It had to be closed after a couple of hours and remains closed at the time of writing, almost a year later. It's the same basic phenomenon. If enough people walk in step, then as their weight shifts from one foot to another in unison that sets up a tiny vibration in the bridge which gets amplified with each succeeding step; so the more it vibrates the bigger the vibrations become. This also explains how singing a high note can shatter a glass: the vibrations of the sound set off vibrations in the atoms of the glass, through resonance, until the atoms vibrate so strongly that they cannot hold together. To sum it up:

> *Any object has a certain natural or resonant*
> *frequency. Strike it, bump it, pluck it, or heat it*
> *and it will tend to vibrate at a specific frequency.*
> *This applies to a bone, a piece of wood, a molecule,*
> *an electron or a musical instrument.*

> James L. Oschman

When we are well, each part of the body will be vibrating at its 'natural or resonant frequency', so it will be working at its best. And that's the way the body as a whole works best too, because then each vibration of each part will be interacting consistently and coherently with all the others. It's a more specific way of saying that all the parts will be in balance. When we feel unwell, or fall ill, that'll be because at least one part is vibrating at the wrong frequency, and even if it is only one part, that vibration will have knock-on effects on all the others and the system as a whole will be thrown off balance. To what degree it is off balance, and how ill you feel, depends on how important the part is and how much its vibration changes. The vibration of the heart is by far the strongest in the body, so if that changes a lot the effects will be widespread and you'll probably feel really ill. By contrast, if there is a small change in the vibration of the stomach you may just have mild nausea. Getting well again is a matter of re-establishing the normal vibration of each part of the body and therefore of the whole. The different techniques of the different energy medicines work by restoring these normal vibrations of the body. Often that is matter of treating the part of the body which set off the chain reaction – once that is back to normal, and the knock-on effects disappear, all the rest will sort themselves out. Sometimes the imbalance is so widespread or so longstanding that all the affected parts will need help to get back to normal.

Vibrations can deviate from their ideal frequency in all sorts of ways. In a person who is listless and depressed, the overall vibration of the energy body will almost certainly have become too weak and will need to be boosted (Figure 12a). If someone has high blood pressure, a red face, and shooting pains in his head, then the vibration of his energy body will probably be too strong and will need calming (Figure 12b). Usually, the state of a person's energy is a bit more complicated; there will be a mixture of some vibrations which are weaker than they should be and others which are stronger (Figure 12c).

Looking a bit more closely at the complex state, imagine that the organs of the body are the dozen employees of a small organization (depending on what you count, there are about a dozen organs). Two or three of these employees aren't pulling their weight; they spend most of the day chatting, drinking tea, and sitting with their feet up on their desks, only getting on with the most urgent jobs, and then only when someone is shouting for them to be done. You could say they have a low vibration. The performance of the organization as a whole will suffer, and so will the others who work there. At least some of those others will be working much harder than usual to keep the show on the road and to cover for their colleagues; you could say they have a high vibration. Of course, it could all have started the other way round. If there are two or three busybody workaholics, constantly interfering with other people's work and taking it over, then those others will get into

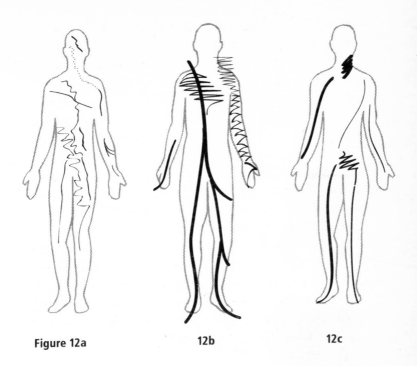

Figure 12a   **12b**   **12c**

the habit of leaving it for them and taking it easy. However it started, the result will be the same. Some employees will be using and giving out lots of energy while others will stir into action reluctantly, feebly and irregularly. It is pretty much the same with the organs. Usually, the vibrations of some will need to be calmed and dispersed while the vibrations of others will need to be jump-started and boosted.

Later in this chapter I will explain how this is done, but first I want to add that there are many more ways, apart from being too strong or too weak, that vibrations can deviate from normal. If a vibration is fragile, small disturbances can knock it out of rhythm. This is a useful way to think of allergies. The affected organ can maintain its normal vibration most of the time, but it is over-sensitive to certain substances, like dust mite, strawberries or pollen. So when pollen comes along it shifts that vibration out of its normal range. It's a bit like a young tree which has been staked on three sides, and is held up against the wind from those directions, but which can be blown over easily by a gust from the fourth. Similarly, some people get stomach upsets as soon as they eat any unaccustomed foods or eat at unusual times; those in whom the vibrations of the stomach are robust can eat kippers and pickled onions, together, at any time of the day or night.

Another kind of deviation from normal is where there is no steady or regular pattern of vibrations; the energy is chaotic. Suppose that this is the case with a person's colon. The result will be very uncomfortable alternating periods of constipation and periods of diarrhoea. And, as the energy of each organ manifests mentally and emotionally as well as physically there will probably be times when that person will cling onto his friends, imposing on them in a way that may feel demanding and needy, and also times when he doesn't make contact and seems not to care. Finally, to take the most extreme example, there can be times in a person's life, usually when he or she has been under some great strain, when all the vibrations of all the organs take on a different rhythm from normal. I have had this experience myself and it felt very peculiar. I didn't feel myself – which in a way was true. After treatment, when my normal vibrations were restored, I said what many people say when they've recovered from an illness, 'I feel myself again'.

Resonance

If two or more things which are in close proximity have a similar vibration, then sooner or later their vibrations will become synchronized. In Figure 13 the two waves represent two vibrations – you can think of them as two notes of music which send sound waves through the air. At the start, on the left-hand side of the figure, they have a very similar wave form, but the peaks and troughs don't quite coincide. As you follow the two towards the right you'll see that they gradually fall more and more into line with each other. This phenomenon is called resonance. It is the explanation for many experiences; some are quick and immediate while others happen over a longer period of time. An example of quick resonance comes from playing stringed instruments. Sound a note on a violin or guitar and if there is another instrument in the same room tuned to the same pitch it will sound the same note on its own, without anyone touching it. In the same way, a number of pendulum clocks mounted on the same wall will eventually become synchronized. Providing the pendula are roughly the same length, start them off in any random order and they will eventually all end up swinging together. An example of resonance over a longer period of time is the way the menstruation of women who live together becomes synchronized. They may start off having their periods at different times of the month, and at different intervals too, but over the course of a few months they gradually converge in both respects.

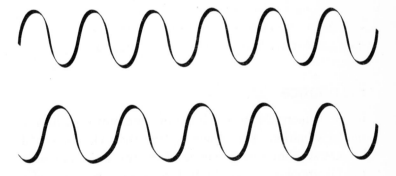

Figure 13

It seems that resonance happens not just between people, but even between individual cells of the body.

> *Place several heart cells together in a dish without any physical contact between one another and with no synapse connecting them and they suddenly fall into a rhythmic unison, a rhythm that is distinct from the rhythm of each individual cell.*

> Paul Pearsall

In the last forty years or so there has been a good deal of scientific research into how this phenomenon of resonance might work in the body. Robert Becker, a pioneer in this field, found that passing a very weak electrical current, at a very specific frequency, through broken bones speeded up their healing considerably, and following his work a number of companies now manufacture simple machines for doing this. In Becker's view, a fracture disturbs the normal vibration of the bone, and it is that vibration which coordinates and manages all the materials and processes of repair. So re-establishing the normal vibration is crucial.

It is done by resonance. The machine introduces a fresh vibration which is at the bone's normal frequency. What happens then is that the bone starts to resonate with the new electrical vibration, and its previously disturbed vibration starts to become synchronized with that of the machine. Once this new vibration has become fully established, you can switch off the machine because the bone can then carry on by itself. Obviously the exact frequency of the machine's vibration is critical; it must be the same as that of bone in its normal undamaged state. Incidentally, that is why it took so long to discover this form of treatment. Before Becker's work, scientists assumed that such weak currents couldn't possibly affect the body, and more generally they thought that the stronger the current the more powerful the effect. That turned out not to be true. Ultrasound treatments, commonplace now especially for sports injuries, are based on this idea.

The theory, then, is that the techniques of energy medicine work by re-establishing the normal vibration in any part of the body which isn't healing, and they do so by introducing a new vibration with which the injured part can resonate. It is only a theory, but it accounts for the examples I've mentioned and there is also some circumstantial evidence which points to the same conclusion. In a series of experiments, people were put in a room which was insulated from the earth's magnetic field. Their body functions went haywire, but were restored to normal when an electric pulse vibrating at a very low frequency was introduced into the room. This suggests all sorts of ideas, but in this context the point is that subjecting people to a vibration at a very low frequency can make their bodies function properly. In another set of experiments measurements were taken of the hands of practitioners of energy medicine who use touch in their work. When the practitioner was at work, the hands emanated a pulsing vibration which varied from 0.3 to 30 Hz, but was at 7-8 Hz most of the time. This is very close indeed to the frequency used in the sealed room experiment. None of this is conclusive, but the evidence is piling up that vibrations at the correct frequency are critical for human healing and that, if disrupted, they can be re-established through resonance.

All this takes me back to the idea that when making a diagnosis a practitioner is looking for the patient's underlying wellness. You may have thought that wellness was a rather vague word, and wondered what it is. In the light of all this, perhaps it is the body's ability to recognize and respond to a correct vibration, by resonance. However ill a person may be, if that ability is unimpaired then healing is possible.

Remedies

A correct vibration can be introduced into the body in a wide variety of ways. It can by done by machines and it can be done by people, stones, colours, sounds, plants, anything which has a suitable vibration. In this section I am going to consider those forms of energy medicine which use methods other than touch.

The way in which colour helps people to get well is pretty straightforward. We all know how awful we feel if we are deprived of natural light for more than a few days. This is now recognized as a kind of depression, known as SAD, or seasonal affective disorder. So severe are the effects that deliberately depriving prisoners of light can amount to torture. This isn't just a psychological issue. Light contains the basic spectrum of colour we see in a rainbow and each colour has a distinct wavelength with a corresponding frequency. Normal life depends on receiving all these colours. Here is a report from a prison cell:

> But wait. My eyes are almost burned by what I see.
> There's a bowl of fruit in front of me that wasn't there
> before. A brown button bowl and in it some apricots,
> some small oranges, some nuts, cherries, a banana.
> The fruits, the colours, mesmerize me in a quiet
> rapture that spins through my head. I am entranced
> by colour. I lift an orange into the flat filthy palm of
> my hand and feel, smell and lick it. The colour
> orange, the colour, the colour, my God the colour
> orange. Before me is a feast of colour. I feel myself
> begin to dance, slowly, I am intoxicated by colour.

> Brian Keenan

So if a particular part or function of the body isn't working well it makes sense to expose it to an extra dose of the particular colour which will resonate with the healthy frequency of that part. Machines have been developed which can do this. More traditionally, practitioners of this kind of energy medicine can detect an aberrant vibration as a disturbed colour in the client's energy body; they then give the client an intense exposure to that colour, whether in the form of liquid, cloth, or a filter over a source of light.

Perhaps this is how healing with stones works too. The light which shines through an emerald will have a different vibration from the light which shines through a ruby, or a diamond, or a quartz crystal. The skill of the practitioner lies in selecting the gem with the appropriate colour for that particular patient. I know very little about rocks and minerals but some time ago I was given a piece of obsidian – a black volcanic rock – by someone who does. She told me it would help me to hold it if I was feeling drained by my work or upset by a patient's predicament. I didn't really believe her, but I tried it a few times and was so impressed with the results that I now use it regularly.

As for sound, it is no accident that I have used it as an analogy so often. It is the most obvious form of vibration and one which we all know well. Every parent knows the power of lullabies for fractious babies. Singing, chanting, and playing musical instruments have accompanied religious ritual from time immemorial, and until the development of scientific medicine, there was no clear distinction drawn between religion and healing. To be sure, the mechanism was not understood; although no one knew quite how it affected the body, no one doubted that it did. So similar are the effects of sound and colour that many practitioners who use one also use the other in some way. The following quotation comes from a famous teacher, who is also a scientist by training:

> To find the pitch for each chakra, I vary the range a
> bit until I hit a resonance. This resonance can be
> heard and felt by the patient. Since I can also see the

> *field [by which she means what I have called the*
> *energy body], I watch the chakra respond to the*
> *sound. When I hit the right pitch the chakra tenses up*
> *and begins to spin rapidly and evenly. Its colour*
> *brightens up. After holding the sound for some time,*
> *the chakra is charged and strengthened enough to hold*
> *its new level of energy.*
>
> *The same principles that are used for sounding into*
> *the chakras also work with the organs and bones of*
> *the body ... for healing injured disks.*

Barbara Ann Brennan

As this quotation shows, with these kinds of techniques it makes little sense to distinguish the organs of the body from its energy flows, such as the chakras. Vibration will resonate with vibration, and what we differentiate as parts or functions or energy flows are simply different frequencies of vibrations in different locations.

Resonance is at the root of all these kinds of energy medicine, and it would be tediously repetitive to say something about each of them separately. But there are three about which I need to say a little more – plants and herbal remedies, homeopathy, and acupuncture.

The way resonance might work with remedies made from plants and herbs is a little more complex and more speculative. Chemists have spent a lot of time and ingenuity analyzing the composition of plants which have traditionally been used to treat certain conditions. Sometimes they find that there is an active ingredient which explains how they work. Foxglove, for example, has long been taken for heart complaints and it is now known that it contains digitalis, which has a powerful chemical effect on the heart. White willow bark was traditionally taken for pain in general and rheumatism in particular;

it contains salicylic acid which is now manufactured and sold as aspirin. Much more often the chemists find nothing that could help, and they dismiss the plant as useless. But is it really plausible that a few of these traditional remedies are valid and most of them are not?

Chemists would certainly dismiss as nonsense the theory which underlies the use of plant remedies. The lichen 'usnea' is prescribed for chronic bronchitis because it grows along the branches of a tree. What is the connection between the way it grows and the illness? If you imagine a tree upside down its branches look remarkably like the tubes of the bronchi. The theory is that something which grows on the bark of the branches will therefore work on the lining of the bronchi. It does seem rather unlikely. Here is another example. Holly essence – one of the Bach's flower remedies – is prescribed for people who are sharp, negative, biting, sarcastic, even vicious. Why? Because if you get entangled in a holly bush it'll claw you unmercifully. So these traditional remedies were found by looking for a match between the patterns in nature and the pattern of an illness. Without some idea of what that match could be, it looks like hocus pocus. But perhaps the nature of the plant speaks of its vibration, as do that patient's symptoms. Then, matching the vibration of the plant to the vibration of the patient will set up a resonance between them.

> The resonance between the plant used as remedy and the person needing it may occur on the level of physiological functioning – where the organizational pattern of the remedy corresponds to something that is wrong with your physical body, such as a wart. It can also occur on mental or spiritual levels, like the trembling of an aspen leaf, which corresponds to the anxiety and shakiness experienced in the mind.

> Dr Rudolph Ballentine

Resonance may also explain something about homeopathy which is particularly puzzling. On the table in front of me there are two small jars of arnica remedies. One is labeled 30C and the other 200C; these figures are known as the potencies. In preparing this remedy a small amount of arnica is mixed with water and a little alcohol and shaken thoroughly. A small part of the resulting mixture is then siphoned off, mixed again with water and alcohol and shaken again. When a remedy has a potency of 200C it means that it has been done two hundred times. What is puzzling, and what induces chemists to shake their heads more in sorrow that in anger, is that the high potency remedies are more powerful than the low ones. In other words, the less arnica there is in the final remedy, the more forcefully it works. It simply isn't possible to say that arnica, or any other homeopathic remedy, works through some active ingredient, like the digitalis in foxgloves. For one thing, there probably isn't any arnica left in the final remedy; and even if there are minute traces, how come less works better?

No-one knows why this is, although there are pointers. Allergens are substances like pollen and house dust mites which cause an allergic reaction in certain people. The normal test for allergies is to prick the skin with a tiny amount of an allergen and see if it brings up a nasty weal; if it does the person is allergic to that substance. Some researchers had the bright idea of following the homeopathic procedure with various allergens. They got people who they knew were allergic to pollen, for example, to hold a glass tube containing utterly diluted pollen. Their eyes went red and itchy, they started sneezing and they showed all the classic signs of an allergic reaction. An explanation for this result is that their energy resonated with the vibrations, not the chemistry, of the pollen. Those vibrations were still, somehow, carried in the water and alcohol and then passed through the glass tube. It may be that the more the mixture is shaken the more the energy of the original substance is released into the water and amplified. It's a bit reminiscent of the fact that very weak electrical currents have a far more powerful effect on the body than stronger ones (at least, until you get to the levels which electrocute people).

Rather less obviously, I think that acupuncture works by resonance too. Each acupuncture point has a highly specific function. It is easy to misunderstand this, as people do when they ask which point is good for headaches or period cramps or stomach ulcers. The function of a point isn't to act on a particular place in the body, it is to bring about a change in the patient's energy. Having decided what energetic change will enable the body to get back into balance – so it can deal with whatever is causing the pain – the acupuncturist then chooses a point, or points, which will bring about that change. A great acupuncturist knows the nature of each point rather as a great gardener knows the nature of each plant or a great chef knows the nature of each ingredient. As with plants and food, every aspect of the point tells a story: where it is on the body, the meridian it belongs to, its place along that meridian and its name all reveal part of its nature. Many of the point names are beautiful and inspiring, for example, Spirit Burial Ground, Bubbling Spring, Palace of Weariness, and they need to be understood both literally and poetically. In short, each point has its own energy, its own vibration. Needling it will stimulate that vibration and the rest of the body can then start to resonate with it. In the words of the heading quote (written by a practitioner who is both an acupuncturist and a herbalist), 'Therapeutic interventions don't cause anything. They resonate with the possibility that was always there.' The needles touch into pockets of wellness, however ill the patient may be, and wellness of a highly specific kind. That is why so many acupuncture patients feel a curious sense of relief during a treatment, even if the needles hurt. It is the relief of having wellness noticed, touched and encouraged.

Touch

There is a whole group of energy medicines which work with or through touch: reflexology, Rolfing, shiatsu, cranio-sacral therapy, zero balancing and Bowen are examples. The physical pressure they use adds a new dimension to treatment.

Because I'm now talking about techniques which, however gentle, do something as down-to-earth as pulling and pushing, I want to use the analogy of clearing a blocked drain. I've tried four methods to shift that wodge of tea leaves, coffee grounds, bits of vegetable peel and solidified fat. I usually start by pouring boiling water down it; with any luck the heat will melt the fat and the block will fall apart into little bits which will be washed away. This rarely works. My next attempt uses suction, one of those rubber things with a handle which you whoosh up and down; if the wodge won't go downwards, maybe it'll go upwards for a moment and that'll break its stranglehold. The next step is chemical; a terrifying liquid which, like all proper magic potions, smokes as you pour it. It ate a spoon I had left in the sink by mistake, so I suppose it devours the wodge (you can tell I'm not a chemist). If this do-it-yourself stuff fails, I get an expert in who pushes a rod through it. These four methods are different in that one uses heat, one suction, one a chemical force and the last uses brute force. What they have in common is that they all use energy of one kind or another.

I've gone into what you might think is excessive detail about my sink because this group of energy medicines works by clearing the blocks in the flows of energy through the body. To shift any block you need to apply a force, or energy, to it which is stronger than the energy which is holding it in place. Of course the body is a lot more complicated than a sink, and an energy block will be held in place by a complex set of energies. Take the neck for example. The interactions of many bones, joints, ligaments and muscles enable the weight of the head to be carried securely and at the same time provide an enormously wide range of movement. If there is a block in the energy flow down the spine, or in the flows through muscle on the top of the shoulder – a tense place for many people – then the neck will be pulled away from its normal alignment. As you can imagine, the forces which will then be operating on the neck will be very confused. Overlaid on the original forces will be a whole set of new ones, some created by the block itself, and others trying to compensate for the block in order to make the best of a bad job. To unblock all this you need to introduce a new stronger force, or more accurately – acknowledging the widespread and three-dimensional nature of the forces involved – a new stronger force field. And it helps the body if the new force field you introduce is clearer than the old one. Clearer in the sense that an ironed shirt is clearer than a creased one, and clearer in the sense of suddenly knowing what to do after you've struggled for ages with a difficult dilemma. Clearer meaning simpler, just right, obvious. Once the clearer stronger force field is applied and the block clears, energy flows again as it should and, often with a gentle kind of flop, everything falls into place again.

If you know how to introduce a clearer, stronger, force field into your own body you won't need a practitioner to do it for you. Yoga, tai chi, and chi gung, as well as the martial arts like aikido and karate, are all based on a highly sophisticated knowledge of the structural and energetic anatomy of the body. Their techniques all create clearer stronger force fields, some in specific joints, some in sections of the body, and some through the whole, and all of them can be used as both preventive and curative medicine. Do yoga teachers ever need treatment then? Yes they do, sometimes, though probably less often than most people. Like all of us, they have their blind spots, and they don't always know what they need. And occasionally, their skill may work against them. As they have the ability to introduce very powerful fields into the body they can cause harm if they misdiagnose what they need, and they may then need someone else to untangle what they've done.

Under the hands of a skilled practitioner it doesn't take long to create a clearer stronger force field. In the early days of my own training I watched Fritz Smith hold a woman's knee gently for about ten seconds – admittedly he had examined it very carefully for about fifteen minutes first. She then got off the couch and had no pain in that knee for the first time for many years, since her Alsatian dog had fallen on it from one side. Anyone would have been astonished; maybe she was a bit more astonished than most because she was a doctor. I last saw her about three years after this treatment and she had had no pain or problem with her knee since then. As with supplying exactly the right resonance, it's a matter of supplying exactly the right force field to the body. In fact, there may not be any difference between the two. The force field of the knee may be simply another way of describing the natural resonant frequency of the knee.

The container

If energy doesn't have a container it leaks away. A treatment works much better if there is no leakage, simply because there will be more energy available to do the work. What constitutes a container is a rich mixture of the physical, the psychological, the emotional and probably much more. At its simplest, treatments don't work well in corridors; the space needs to be enclosed and private and pretty soundproof. I sometimes treat people in their own homes, but it doesn't usually work as well as in my treatment room; however nice the room and however quiet it is, I think the patient's awareness of the life of the house, and his or her associations with things in the room, means that some energy leaks away. I try not to leave the room during a treatment because I think it can break the container too. Confidentiality is part of this too; information that is shared in the room stays in the room.

All this applies to any system of medicine, but it is especially important in energy medicine because treatment seeks to move the client's energy in a deliberate and specific way. If the patient is busy trying to get comfortable, panicking about what is going on, trying to damp down emotions which are surfacing, chatting, or writing letters in his or her head, there will be that much less energy available for change. Cooking provides a good analogy. Things cook more quickly in a pan with the lid on than in a pan without a lid. The energy of the heat is contained and amplified if it is enclosed. Quickest of all is a pressure cooker. The practitioner needs to put the lid on things, so to speak. It is done in a hundred ways, and I suspect that most of them are unconscious. At particularly powerful times of change one practitioner I know will sit at the head of the treatment couch and hold the patient's shoulders, quite firmly but neutrally. Another will pull up a chair and sit alongside the couch; she doesn't talk, she gets very still and even closes her eyes. The stillness provides a kind of container; it encourages the patient to be still too and allow what is happening to happen without interruption. Another practitioner will talk her patient through the shifts in energy, rather like a river guide talking beginners through the rapids; that too keeps the energy from dissipating into something else or somewhere else. In one of my own treatments I found myself puffing out my breath forcefully and noisily; the practitioner advised me to stop doing that as I was 'letting off steam' rather than 'using it to cook'.

For all that the practitioner can do to help, the most powerful container is the one which only the patient can provide. It is the container which is created by a kind of focused attention. If the patient really pays attention to what is happening in the body and exactly where it is happening, and refuses to be distracted, then remarkable things can happen.

There are all sorts of stories about this phenomenon in other walks of life. There are reports of parents who, in the stress of the moment, have managed to lift unbelievable weights to free their trapped children. Of people who, in deep meditation, not only manage appalling pain, but don't even feel it. Or, to take a rather more everyday example, of a golfer whose drive, at a crucial moment in a tournament, flew straight down the fairway even though there was a loud whistle from a passing train just as he was swinging. When questioned afterwards about how he managed to hit such a good shot in spite of the sudden noise, he is said to have asked, in all innocence, 'what noise?' The many kinds of visualization techniques, in which people see their white blood cells gobbling up infections or their bones knitting after a fracture, all depend on this power of focused attention. As one doctor said to his patient, a Zen Master, at his annual check-up, 'Your blood pressure is a little high. Could you do whatever it is you do to bring it down?'

Mysteries

Not every treatment works well, or at all. At one time, I analyzed the records of treatments I had given over the previous few years. About six patients out of ten got completely better from whatever it was that was troublesome enough to get them to turn up, and another two or three reported at least a considerable improvement. What was going to be really inter-esting and useful, I thought, would be the records of the ones who didn't get better. They should show me my mistakes, or, almost as helpful actually, they would show me the conditions I couldn't help with. So if someone with that condition were to ring up in future I could simply say that I hadn't had any success in their kind of case (someone else might) and save their time and money. However, the results showed none of the patterns I expected. For one thing, success or failure had nothing to do with belief in the treatment. An elderly man who, when he turned up for every appointment announced to the whole clinic in a very loud voice, 'I don't believe in this malarkey you know' (he wasn't teasing, he really didn't), recovered completely from a very serious complaint which, according to his doctors, was incurable. On the other hand, a couple of patients who believed passionately in complementary medicine showed no improvement at all. Nor did it seem to have anything to do with how long the problem had been going on. A middle-aged woman turned up telling me she'd had a migraine every ten days or so for twenty years and after three treatments they were gone for good: her son had had a slightly stiff neck after a night on a transatlantic flight the previous week and, try as I might, I made no difference to it whatever. Frustratingly, some of the patients I got on best with didn't get well and others who I found difficult improved in leaps and bounds. My researches were a failure – or perhaps they were a success in that they taught me yet again how little we understand of the awesome complexity of another human being.

To sum up, quite a lot of this chapter has been speculative, in the sense that I cannot say authoritatively how a treatment works. Still, I think there is good evidence for what I have written, and everything I've said is entirely consistent with my own experience both as a practitioner and as a patient. This may be as much as we can reasonably expect. In the end, every patient is an individual and however much is known about a particular drug or operation or remedy or herb, not everyone will respond to it in the same way. All we can do is to work as honestly as possible, knowing that there are limitations to our knowledge. A patient's psoriasis doesn't improve: was that because the treatment didn't work, or would it have got worse if she hadn't had treatment? You'll never know. A patient's arthritis clears up completely: was that because of the treatment or in spite of the mistakes of the practitioner? You'll never know. And it may be wiser not to pretend we can ever fully understand how treatments work. If we think we can, that may lead us into an arrogance which closes our minds to learning more and learning better what will help those who are ill. An eminent scientific researcher wrote:

> Medical techniques have come to be tested as much against current concepts in biochemistry as against their empirical results. Techniques that don't fit such chemical concepts – even if they seem to work – have been abandoned as pseudoscientific or downright fraudulent.

Robert O. Becker and Gary Selden

This applies just as much to energy medicine and its practitioners. The reality is always more complex than the theory, the treatment is always an approximation, and every patient's route to recovery is a unique creative act.

Chapter 7

What 'working' means

I watched a six-year-old girl with cerebral palsy balance herself on her knees for the first time, supported only at the hips. She gave such a cry of joy at this sensation that no other medical corroboration was needed.

Ted Kaptchuk and
Michael Croucher

How can you tell if a treatment has worked? It's a crucial question, not only for each individual patient but for any system of medicine. At first sight, the answer is obvious – the pain has gone away, the symptoms have disappeared, and all is as it was before. But this answer just isn't good enough. For one thing, the illness might have cleared up by itself, without any medical intervention; for all you know, it might have been cleared up more quickly and more effectively. In evaluating any treatment, you can't ignore this possibility – there are plenty of stories of people who heal on their own, without any kind of medicine, even from apparently incurable illnesses. So if you've had a treatment, and got better, you'll never know for sure if it was the treatment that made the difference; you can't live that period of your life over again without the treatment to see what happens.

When a new drug is tested, researchers try to get round this problem by carrying out what are called double blind trials. A large number of patients are given the new drug and the same number of other patients, carefully selected to be similar in all sorts of ways to the original group, are given something that looks just like the drug but is simply sugar or coloured water or something of the sort. Then the recovery rates of the two groups are compared. If the first group does significantly better, then the researchers conclude that the drug works. That is all well and good, but it does leave out exactly what an individual patient wants to know – whether or not a particular drug will work for him or her. In other words, statistics deal with generalities and probabilities, and the person who is ill wants specifics. When you are ill you want to be regarded as an individual and you want to have a treatment which is tailored to you; you're not interested in what that treatment does on the whole or by and large, nor in what it might do for someone else. Instinctively, and correctly, you feel that although you are like other people in many ways you are also unique, and so is your illness. And you know that although a drug may work well for many people with similar symptoms to yours, it may not work for you.

And there is another problem in evaluating the effects of treatment. Sometimes a treatment seems to make the symptoms worse for a while before they get better. There are lots of examples where it is pretty clear that aggravated symptoms are really part of the process of healing. Fever, for example, is essentially the body's own way of destroying threatening micro-organisms; if a treatment raises body temperature that is probably benign, helping the body to heal quickly and safely. If you stop smoking or drinking alcohol or coffee, you usually get some quite unpleasant symptoms as the body rids itself of the accumulated toxins – but no one doubts that giving up these things is healthy. All this is especially relevant with energy medicine. A homeopath may expect a patient's symptoms to get worse, in some ways and temporarily, as the remedy takes effect. A patient may feel more pain after a treatment. As the energy body reorganizes, the joints, muscles and ligaments, or the organs and their interrelationships, will need time to adjust to the new situation and they may complain, so to speak, at having to cope with new pressures and unaccustomed flows of energy. We all get set in our ways, even if they are ways that aren't particularly good for us, and we tend to make a fuss if we are asked to change; the body is no different. And, as I have said before, when deep-seated illnesses start to heal they often retrace the stages by which they were driven deep into the body. Therefore, along with the deep healing, which may be almost imperceptible on a daily or even weekly basis, the patient may have all sorts of new symptoms. So a treatment that is really effective and powerful may seem to be making things worse – and it isn't always easy to decide if it is or not.

When you are ill you want to get back to the way you were before – so getting back to normal seems to be a test of whether or not a treatment has worked. That's clearly true in the case of simple occasional illnesses, like catching a cold or the flu. But with a more serious illness, or one which keeps coming back, it isn't at all clear that getting back to normal really helps. If you have been living in a way that virtually guarantees illness sooner or later – eating poor food on the run, wearing the kind of shoes that strain the hips, never getting enough sleep, being in an unhappy relationship, or working at a job you hate – and routinely ignoring warning signs of impending trouble, then illness can be a boon. It may well be the body's way of telling you to stop living that way; the body's way of giving you an opportunity to stop and reconsider. For some people, being told the truth about the causes of their illness will be an important part of their treatment; so too, if they choose to make the necessary and often difficult changes in their lives, will be getting the energy, support and encouragement to help them to do so. In this kind of case, a treatment which allows a person to get back to where they were, can't really be said to 'work'.

In short, the whole business of knowing whether or not a treatment has worked isn't simple. To some extent this is true of any system of medicine, but it is a particularly acute issue in the case of energy medicine. There are a number of reasons for this. One of them is that conventional medicine works so quickly that the link between cause and effect seems straightforward; the cortisone injection into a painful elbow brings immediate relief, the removal of a cancerous tumour halts the spread of the disease (though only time will tell if these treatments are long lasting). With energy medicine, changes are usually slower and less dramatic and hence less easy to attribute to the treatment. I want to look first at how to assess whether or not an energy medicine treatment is working; as you will see, that raises the wider issue of what it means to be well.

Functions and potential

Unless something goes wrong we all take the state of our basic functions for granted. Someone who doesn't have the slightest trouble getting to sleep probably never thinks twice about it whereas the chronic insomniac is grateful for the rare occasions when sleep comes easily. The same is true for all those who have no difficulty with their breathing, posture, movement, eating, menstruation, temperature or bowels. Offhand, I can't think of a single example of a patient I have treated who hasn't had problems with one of these functions, even if the main complaint doesn't appear to involve it at all. For example, I am treating a young woman whose hair is falling out; she also has irregular and painful periods. I see many people with breathing problems who are also constipated. Those whose digestion doesn't work reliably usually have weak musculature and poor posture; if the body slumps there is pressure on the relevant organs and they literally don't have room to function properly. If I treat someone whose legs have become weak, through injury or chronic illness, I usually have to do something to help their poor circulation; the leg muscles play a key role in getting blood to flow back up the body to the heart. The body is made up of unimaginably complex interrelationships, and a weakness in one function will affect others. It follows that the opposite is true too; if one system gets stronger, works more efficiently and becomes more robust, then the other systems will respond. Say a patient has symptoms on the skin – acne, eczema or rashes – and starts to have treatment for that complaint with some form of energy medicine. After two or three sessions there is no sign of change on the skin. Is it worth persisting with treatment or not? A good test is to compare the current state of the basic systems with how they were before treatment started. If the patient reports an improvement in his or her breathing I can be pretty sure that it is working; as I have mentioned before, the energy of the skin and the lungs are very closely related. I'd reach the same conclusion if the patient told me that he was no longer constipated; the colon is also linked with lungs and skin. I would be less sure, but still confident, if the result of treatment was that the patient slept better or found that she no longer minded the cold, or realized that her digestion had improved; none of these functions are specifically associated with the skin, but still, the better everything works the more energy there is available for healing the skin.

It takes a lot of energy to keep any system going if it isn't working properly. One of the ways in which I find out how someone is when they first come to see me, is by moving their joints gently to see how flexible they are. You would be amazed at how much energy people use to keep their arms, legs, hips, and necks stiff and held in place. With one young woman I saw recently I lifted both her feet about three inches off the couch and stretched her legs very gently – I was seeing how energy flowed through her structure. When I took my hands away, expecting her feet to flop back down on the couch, they stayed at exactly the same height. They'd probably have stayed there throughout the whole treatment if I hadn't asked her to put them down. Imagine the effort it took to do that – and she was entirely unaware that she had done it or, when I mentioned it to her, that there was anything odd or unusual about it. She is an extreme example, but to a lesser degree, most of the people I see, constantly drain their energy by holding their bodies in strange and forced ways. Holding emotions in place gobbles up energy too. As I've mentioned before, the natural flow of the energy of anger is to come upwards and outwards in the body. If, for some reason, it is impossible or unacceptable to express that anger, then it must be held in, and it needs the equivalent of reinforced concrete to do so. Some people do it for so long that it distorts their posture badly; you can see it when they walk in the room. There's a tremendous stiffness in the middle of the body, at the level of the diaphragm. It tends to throw their chest outwards and push the shoulders and neck back. Other people cope by denying that they are angry, but let it out in dribs and drabs through nagging criticism, manipulative behaviours and more or less permanent complaints about their grievances. They feel powerless and hopeless and their posture is drooped; they have caved in, emotionally and physically.

As these examples indicate, the stresses and strains people are under are normally the result of their best efforts to cope; to continue to function in spite of skeletal misalignment, muscular tension, poorly functioning organs, emotional pain and so on. That means, on the one hand, that their efforts to cope must be respected and not regarded as 'something wrong'. It also means, on the other, that if people start to change through treatment, start to relax and release, then there will be an enormous increase in their potential. This potential can then be used for clearing up eruptions on the skin, but it can also be used in a limitless number of other ways too. If there is no pressing physical problem, then it can be harnessed to make dreams come true. That sounds a bit sentimental, but how many people live wishing they could do the work they would love, have closer relationships with their partners or children, feel more kind towards themselves, worry less about their weight – or even fulfil a challenge such as sailing to the Caribbean or climbing the Matterhorn? I'm not saying that a course of treatment will automatically make dreams come true, but a major reason people don't manage to live their dreams is that they will entail changes which are awkward and which therefore demand time, attention and determination. It is an awful lot easier to find these resources in yourself if you have plenty of energy.

What you didn't know you had

All this explains why the first appointment with a practitioner of energy medicine usually takes an hour or more. He or she will want to know how all these basic functions are working, even if they seem to be irrelevant to the patient's complaint, because that information provides a baseline against which to assess the course of treatment. As a patient, it is easy to forget what pain or discomfort was like once it has eased. I've often seen people who, after three or four sessions, say they aren't much better. Then I look back at the notes I made at the first session and remind them of what they told me: then they say 'oh yes, I'd forgotten that. It does feel better.' Even more satis-fying, and even more telling, is when someone reports to me after a few sessions that, for example, their headaches have stopped or that they now have regular and easy periods and I don't remember that problem. I check the notes I took in the first session and, sure enough, there's no mention of it. This is not a criticism. People forget, or they are embarrassed to talk about some things at a first meeting, or they are so used to living with something the way it is they can't see any point in mentioning it; in any case, they see it as a separate issue, so it must be irrelevant. Still, if a problem I didn't even know about has improved, I take it as a sure sign that treatment is working. It's the same point again: if energy is better balanced the body will sort itself out.

Another reason people don't mention what is wrong with them is that they are coping and they don't realize how much better they could feel.

> At the end of a series of sessions, I try to get feedback from my clients. I need to know what is working for people and what isn't. One of the first times I did this was with a powerful woman lawyer. During the last session I said to her very formally, 'I thought it would be a good idea to review what happened here.'
>
> 'That would be wonderful,' she said.
>
> 'Grand,' I said. 'I'd like to ask you, did you get what you came for?'
>
> She replied, 'Absolutely not.'
>
> I was flabbergasted. I asked what she meant.
>
> She said, 'Rachel, when I came here I didn't know that what I had even existed.'
>
> Rachel Naomi Remen

Once the whole body, with its manifold energy flows, is engaged in a treatment, then what happens may go far beyond the obvious business of removing a particular pain or easing a specific discomfort. What people originally report as the problem isn't what concerns them the most. Maybe they don't even know what's wrong, really.

... I approach Don José and ask him to perform a healing on me.

'What's your problem, sonny?' he asks.

'I've got hay fever.'

'What's that?'

'You know ... allergies,'

'Never heard of them.'

'Well sometimes my eyes get itchy and my nose runs and I sneeze a lot.'

'All right, come by my house in the morning.'

The next morning I present myself at his hut ... At length he pronounces his diagnosis of the cause of my hay fever. 'You've got a girlfriend on the side, huh?'

'No, Don José, I haven't been with anyone else since I've been married.'

... 'Nope, you've got a girlfriend on the side. Sorry, sonny, don't mean to offend you; I'm just telling you what I'm seeing ... Hey, you are a serious case! Your pistol is about to drop off!'...

I notice no effect whatsoever from his treatment, but the next morning I dutifully return to his home where I am treated to the same routine as the day before. This time he seems satisfied with his work. He draws himself up to his full height and declares, 'There! You're clean!'

... Once again I notice no effect. I am dejected. I have come all this way for nothing. Tomorrow I start my journey back home. When night-time comes I can't

*sleep ... Don José's words come to mind: 'You have a
girlfriend on the side.' For the first time I admit to
myself that in a hidden corner of my heart I never let
go of the lover I had before I met my wife. That lover
has been inside me, gnawing like a worm in an apple.
'Your pistol is about to drop off.' An overstatement,
maybe, but for sure the situation has been robbing
some of my sexual energy. Well, okay, a lot of my
sexual energy ... 'Now you are clean!' That is exactly
how I feel ... I feel as clear and energetic as a baby.
My heart fills with love for my wife.*

*Two days later when I reach home, I am still full of
love. My wife receives me at the door. She looks into
my eyes and knows the ghost is gone. In this moment
we wed.*

Eliot Cowan

He doesn't say what happened to his hay fever. That problem
wasn't nearly as important as the one he didn't realize he had.
Although this is a rather dramatic example, much the same
happens with many patients. The original problem may not be
any better, but you can't therefore jump to the conclusion that
the treatment hasn't worked. It may have worked better than
anyone could have expected.

Attitudes to pain and suffering

What I have said so far opens up another aspect of what it
means to say that a treatment has worked, and that has to do
with the patient's attitude to him or herself and to the illness.
One common effect of treatment is that people start to become
more aware of the body and its needs. It is remarkable how
ignorant we are, as a culture, of basic anatomy and physiology.

I spent a long time on the phone the other day with a young man who had torn a ligament playing rugby and wanted me to treat him. The reason the conversation went on so long is that it took me some time to get him to accept that it just had to heal and that nothing that I, nor anyone else, could do would make a lot of difference. I see people with digestive problems, and I know that if I ate what they do, and in the way they do, I would have digestive problems too. I think that one of the benefits of energy medicine is that it educates people – and it doesn't do so by hectoring or exhortation, which is normally ignored, but by giving people a real body-felt sensation of what is going on inside. If you've felt the relief spreading through your whole body as energy starts to flow again through the sacroiliac joint, you'll be more careful of how you bend and twist in the future and you'll know to seek help more quickly if it gets jammed up again. To take another example, I don't treat people who come to me because they want to stop smoking; I know that no treatment I can give them will do it for them. But I do treat people who want to get well and who also smoke. I know that once they have had the sensation of their lungs responding more easily and naturally to each breath they take, even if it is only for a few minutes in the treatment room, then it becomes very much easier for them to choose not to smoke.

These examples imply, again, an interaction between mind and body. I have a patient who came to me because she suffered from bad migraines, which she had regularly and for many years. If you were to ask her if the treatment had got rid of the migraines she would say 'no'. Then she would add something like, ' although the migraines haven't gone away, I now know what brings them on, so if I feel one starting up I just do what I have to and it goes away.' In her case, what she has to do is to eat properly again and go for a long walk with her husband to catch up with each other's lives. Of course, this isn't always practicable, at short notice. But what she has discovered is that if she promises herself that she will do it within a reasonable time, the migraine accepts that, so to speak, and goes away. It sounds odd to say so, but it has learned to trust that she will keep her promise, and it doesn't mind waiting a while. She now sees the migraines as a knot in her handkerchief; a reminder of what she has to do. On a questionnaire, it might look as if the treatment has failed, but she regards it as a success.

These kinds of changes in attitude make all the difference. There is a well-known saying, 'pain is inevitable, but suffering is optional'. The sensation of physical or emotional pain doesn't usually change, whatever attitude you take to it; but that isn't what is hardest to bear. There are people who are in a lot of physical pain but who manage, somehow, to regard it not as an aberration but as a part of being alive as a human being. They may be prevented from leading the life they used to lead, even prevented from doing things they love, but they manage to extract pleasures from the simplest things and to rejoice in sights and sounds which the rest of us hardly notice. I had a friend who was dying in hospital, all through the most beautiful spring I can remember. Through her window she could see the trees outside turning green, see the clarity of the air at that time of the year, and she insisted that all her visitors shared in her appreciation. I saw the spring through her eyes, and could see in her face the way she felt joy and pain and grief simultaneously. Even though there was a lot of pain, she didn't have to be miserable. Thanks to her, practically every morning I delight in being in my own bed with my soft duvet and pillows – it was a pleasure she had noticed she missed in the hospital.

I see many people whose physical complaint, whatever it is, seems really to be a consequence of having had their heart broken. It is very common and some people suffer terribly. They find life pointless, don't want to eat, can't respond to beauty or laughter, find it too much effort to play with children, and avoid company. They endlessly replay how good their life would have been if only the loved one were still around, if only a parent had been kinder, if only they hadn't been betrayed. Their suffering is enormous and takes all their attention. And there are others who may have experienced a similar level of pain, but who don't suffer as much. Although they may feel the pain each day, after a while they manage to do something else as well and to have periods when they aren't suffering. Without being falsely cheerful, they can even come to see the silver lining and to appreciate the benefits which have flowed from what happened. They wouldn't wish to experience that level of pain again, but they can see how it led them to something valuable which they might not have found any other way. This is the sense in which the Christian church talks about 'suffering as grace'. As Ram Dass adds, it is a 'heavy grace'.

So one way of finding out if a treatment has worked is to ask not whether it has alleviated the pain but whether it has alleviated the suffering. As with practically everything I've said so far, it is not something which is easy to capture on a questionnaire. Nor is it all that easy to explain how it is that a treatment can reduce suffering – although I know it can. The nearest I can come to it is to mention again the idea that a treatment can touch and resonate with a person's underlying wellness; a part that hasn't got the depression or the cancer, but just is him or her, as he or she always has been. I think most of us recognize this part of us, even if we aren't normally aware of it in daily life. I know there is a part of me which, whatever I'm doing or feeling in the moment, is the same as it was when I was a little boy, has actually never changed, and as far as I can tell from the eyes of my ninety-year-old father which look the same as they did in a photograph taken when he was about six, never will change. Whatever my body happens to be going through at the moment, that part of me is the same. If a treatment manages to reach that level of a person, then it gives them a different perspective on illness and pain. It opens a door to the possibility of feeling all right in spite of them.

There is one particular way in which this can happen in a treatment. A substantial shift in the state of a patient's energy state can bring about a change in his or her consciousness, with the effect that normal everyday reality disappears and another reality takes its place for a while, one in which the patient experiences a state of timelessness and perfection. It sounds a bit new age, but the basic mechanism was well described in 1901 in a lecture at Edinburgh University given by the American philosopher and psychologist, William James (brother of the more famous Henry). He wrote:

> *our normal waking consciousness … is but one*
> *special type of consciousness, whilst all about it,*
> *parted from it by the filmiest of screens, there lie*
> *potential forms of consciousness entirely different.*
> *We may go through life without suspecting their*
> *existence; but apply the requisite stimulus, and at*
> *a touch there they are in all their completeness …*

William James

This isn't an unusual phenomenon. Lots of people have had experiences of other forms of consciousness, other realities, often when they were supremely happy or supremely sad – states which certainly entail a substantial shift in energy. They can also have them after they've taken drugs or been without food or sleep for a long time, and these too can change the state of a person's energy quite dramatically. They report the results in remarkably similar terms. Here is an example from fiction, though it is hard to believe the author wasn't drawing on some such experience of her own:

> *She felt her arm fall heavy on the table and she*
> *wondered, oddly, whether or not the table objected.*
> *And was the lamp, clamped there to the table's edge,*

exhausted after so long a day? Were the floorboards
reasonably cheerful or the door numb with lack of
movement?

Because now her thoughts flowed through every object
and every corner in the room, and a moment later she
became the walls and also the clean roof overhead and
the powerful black sky. Why, she wondered aloud,
had she stayed so long enclosed by the tough, lonely
pronoun of her body when the whole world beckoned?

Carol Shields

Sometimes an energy medicine treatment will provide the
'requisite stimulus' to access a different state of consciousness,
a different reality. For a time, in that state, the patient may well
not have the pain, the discomfort, the anxiety of illness; they
all exist in the former reality, and aren't experienced by the
altered consciousness. The point, in this context, is that such
experiences can change a patient's attitude to his or her illness.
Having once known that lying in bed in pain isn't the only
reality, that it is possible not to be 'enclosed by the tough
lonely pronoun of her body', then there is a kind of release and
escape from the current condition. While a person is in that
different state of consciousness the pain itself may disappear
for a few moments, but even if it doesn't, the suffering dimin-
ishes. Suffering, at root, is mental. It is a preoccupation with
wanting things to be different; a desperate desire for the pain to
go away or for what you had before you were ill. An experience
of the kind I am describing loosens the grip of these preoccu-
pations, gives a breathing space, allows you to stand apart from
your illness and to define yourself not only as an ill person but
as the self you have always known. It is difficult for me to
convey the power of this, so here is a moving report:

Recently I [was] with a fellow in his mid-thirties who was in the final stages of ALS, also known as Lou Gehrig's disease. When we met, he had no voluntary control over any part of his body except his facial muscles. He communicated by code, pursing his lips for a dot and raising his eyebrows for a dash. The first time I sat by his bedside and we 'talked', I was aware ... of an intense feeling of claustrophobia ... I had difficulty not identifying with him, living inside that crippled body ... but as I quieted down and sat there, my hand resting in his hand, we fell into a deep silence. When I opened my eyes, he spelled out with his face the words, 'Much light, much peace.'

Ram Dass

Energy medicine and conventional medicine

No system of medicine works for everyone or for every complaint. Part of the skill, actually part of the ethical responsibility of any practitioner, is to make sure that the patient gets the most appropriate form of treatment; if necessary by referring him or her to someone else, to some other form of medicine, if that offers a better chance of success. There are many things conventional medicine can do, particularly with acute conditions, which energy medicine can't, and a significant proportion of my long-term patients have needed some form of conventional medicine from time to time. Plenty of people faced with a serious illness use both systems of medicine at the same time; in these kinds of cases, a good test of how well energy medicine is working is how well it complements conventional medical treatment.

The use of a steroid inhaler during an asthma attack, for example, can be a lifesaver. Once the attack is over, what I often find is that the rib cage doesn't work very well. With each breath, each rib lifts, moves outwards, and rotates around its axis, a very complex movement made possible by the flexible joints where each rib meets the spine. The force of an asthma attack can strain those joints quite badly, as can the muscular tension brought on by the patient's fear, and as a result the whole rib cage gets seized up. And that, of course, makes breathing difficult. It is easy, then, to get locked in a spiral of more and more difficult breathing and more and more use of the inhaler. Energy medicine can restore the smooth flow of energy through those joints, and that acts rather like lubricating oil in a car engine. As they start to free up, the rib cage as a whole starts to regain its flexibility, breathing becomes easier and the vicious circle has been halted and put in reverse. If, in the days and weeks after an attack, the patient is breathing better and using his inhaler less and less, then it is fair to believe that the treatment has worked.

It is pretty much the same story with operations. One of my daughters, who had a nasty spiral fracture of her lower leg, needed an operation to reset the bone and the doctors reckoned she'd be in plaster for six months. With regular and intensive energy medicine – there are times when it is useful to have a father who does this kind of work – she was out of plaster in two. What the energy medicine had done, all it had done, was to speed up the healing. It couldn't for a moment have replaced the work of the orthopaedic surgeons. Sometimes the best time for the energy medicine is before an operation. A forty-year-old patient of mine with a severe heart condition had quadruple heart bye-pass surgery a year ago. He had to wait some months for the operation and during that time he had treatment practically every day. He also did a lot of work with a psychotherapist, looking at the psychological issues which this brought to the surface – and which indeed might have had a part to play in the insistent deterioration of his arteries. He didn't expect the operation to do everything, to fix him. He knew he needed it to deal with the accumulated effects of years of failing to look after his health and failure to deal with some vital emotional issues; and he also knew that he would have to get healthy, physically and psychologically, both to get through the operation as easily as possible and to make sure that he wouldn't need it again. He recovered quickly from the operation and is now fit and well.

This kind of collaboration is especially important for those patients who have needed repeated treatment with conventional medicine. Operations to remove polyps from the womb or a cancerous tumour, or to sew up a perforated colon, can again be lifesavers. But what if the patient needs the same operation again three years later? And three years after that? Surely then, you have to think that cutting out or sewing up the tissue isn't tackling the root of the problem; that whatever is causing the polyps to grow, the cancer to recur, the colon to perforate, needs attention. Perhaps surgery and drugs together can deal with both aspects of the problem; but normally conventional medicine isn't so good at helping with long-term chronic conditions, and in the case of recurring problems it looks as if there is an underlying chronic condition. Equally, there are people whose polyps have melted away, whose cancerous cells have reverted to normal after energy medicine treatments, but it is a less reliable method than surgery and if the problem is acute the treatment usually works too slowly. Patients with these kinds of complaints shouldn't need to choose between the two systems; they almost certainly need both.

Knowing

It is hard enough to assess a single simple treatment; once you start to combine different treatments it becomes impossible. From a research point of view, the constellation of interventions and body changes are so complicated and interrelated you simply can't know what caused what. Any kind of objective test goes out of the window. From a patient's point of view, that doesn't matter a damn; all that matters is that he or she gets better. But the difficulty comes when choosing what treatments to have, and whether or not to persist in them. A doctor or practitioner can make recommendations, explain the theory behind what he or she proposes to do, give an honest assessment of whether or not the treatment seems to be working, but cannot give guarantees. The patient embarks on a course of treatment as an explorer embarks on a voyage of discovery. There may be maps, but they are only one of the resources needed for the expedition, and they don't ensure success.

In the end, the patient has to trust his or her own intuition, to trust that gut feeling which says 'this is right for me' or which says 'no' in spite of any logical and sensible arguments to the contrary. That may seem an awfully flimsy basis on which to make important decisions, but two wise phrases suggest otherwise. One is the old saw, 'The heart has reasons the mind knows not of'. The other is a splendidly magisterial put-down given by a Victorian judge to a barrister who had pointed out that the judge's decision was illogical. 'Logic,' said the judge, 'is a way of going wrong with confidence.'

And there can be a moment when all the theories, all the tests, all the medical expertise, and all the doubts are supremely irrelevant. The patient, the practitioner, and anyone else who has the privilege of witnessing the moment knows that the treatment has worked.

> I watched a six-year-old girl with cerebral palsy balance herself on her knees for the first time, supported only at the hips. She gave such a cry of joy at this sensation that no other medical corroboration was needed .

Ted Kaptchuk and Michael Croucher

Conclusion

Patients

...the spirit is the life of the body seen from within, and the body, the outward manifestation of the life of the spirit – the two being really one.

C.G. Jung

I see a huge variety of people. Most have already taken their ailments to their GP repeatedly and have seen a specialist of some kind; quite a lot of them have had operations which haven't worked. They only come to me because they are desperate, frightened, and exhausted from trying one test after another, one procedure after another. Either they are in physical pain, or their normal bodily functions aren't working properly, or they have some condition like hair loss or skin blemishes which makes them feel ugly or unattractive. They sometimes say that they feel rotten or that they don't feel themselves, which are often the only ways they can tell me that their heart has been broken or they are depressed. There's a sort of devastation about them, and it often has to do with something they are ashamed and embarrassed to admit. They have strange symptoms, feel emotions that make no sense to them, or sleep and wake at peculiar times. Their faces have vivid colours or rings under their eyes. I listen to what each one has to say, and I try to sense the flow of his or her life. Usually, this involves getting some feeling for that person's true potential and the way it has been stifled or thwarted, leaving him or her feeling purposeless, fragmented, unsatisfied. I look both for the patterns of their illness and for the patterns of their wellness. I want to soothe the one and stimulate the other at the same time.

That's not the same as curing them, far less healing them. Only their own innate healing system or healing ability can do that. My belief is that if I, or another practitioner of energy medicine, can balance their energy that will provide an opportunity for the patient's own healing power to get to work. I can't force it to do so, and nor can the patient, though he or she can certainly do a lot to help it along. Whether or not patients do help it along is up to them. This isn't a criticism of those who don't: I have struggled with illness myself and I know that a person can consciously want to get better, just as a man with a broken leg may consciously want to run a marathon, but simply not have the resources to do what is needed. Or someone can sincerely want to get better but not realize that what he or she is doing is stopping the healing system from working properly. Or they don't appreciate the power of some old attitude or belief. As a child, for example, a person may have got loving attention only when he or she was ill; now, as an adult, that pattern is still at work and the person falls ill in order to get loving attention. These are only three examples of the hundreds of reasons why people don't heal, and with a particular patient it is unlikely that I will ever fully know or understand what they are. They are probably a complex combination of the mechanical, the chemical, the mental, the emotional and the spiritual. I know too that, as with all things, there is a time for change and it may not be now. If I keep on treating someone, I trust that I am helping, through building up the necessary resources, by being an interested companion at a difficult time, and by ensuring that I will be there to provide the opportunity again when he or she is ready.

Any cure or any healing involves a change from one state to another, and making a change is an effort; the bigger the change, the more effort is needed. The practitioner can play a part in supporting that effort and in helping it to have the most far-reaching effects. But it is the patient who must make the effort to change – no one can do it for him or her.

This applies at all levels, from the simplest to the most profound. At the simplest level, the patient must be willing to make the effort to turn up for treatment. One patient's fingers go blue and become painful whenever it gets cold. It's a chronic condition. He has three or four treatments in October and November and it starts to get better; then he misses the next one. I don't hear from him until after Christmas and then he rings up again for another appointment, rather shame-facedly, because his condition has worsened. We then go through the whole cycle again. He just won't come regularly and give the treatment a chance to make a lasting difference. A similar example is a woman who suffers badly from consti-pation and who is also badly dehydrated. Well, the constipation won't ever get better unless she drinks enough water, but she never does. Instead she comes to me, also irreg-ularly, because she has a week or two of relief afterwards. These may seem to be trivial examples, but the general pattern is very common. With these patients I have to shift my focus. The energetic imbalance I have to address first isn't the one which is resulting in cold fingers or constipation, but the one which somehow makes them unable to do what they know is good for them. It also helps me to stay willing to help. Instead of getting irritated and writing them off as hopeless cases I can treat their inability to help themselves as the illness itself.

At a rather more complex level, take the example of a patient who keeps getting bronchitis and chesty coughs. As he well knows, essentially this is because he is still grieving a rela-tionship which ended some years ago. He can't just stop grieving by an act of will and magically be free of the illness. Equally, he won't get better if he keeps on seeing himself as a victim, nursing his grievances, imagining each day how his life ought to be, and generally shutting himself off from new experiences and relationships. The particular effort he will have to make – it may well be different for someone else – is to feel his grief fully and find out what it is actually like, what it really amounts to; that in itself will change the state he is in. And he'll also have to make the effort to get out and have a social life again. Not easy, and he'll certainly need all the resources he can muster to do it. Having enough energy is one important resource. But no one else can get over his loss for him.

This example makes a general point. If I had to choose one thing a person could best do to help him or herself recover from an illness I would say it is to pay the illness the closest possible attention. I don't mean by this that the patient should become obsessed with ailments and complaints, worrying endlessly over what drugs to take, what new specialist to go to, believing that it can be fixed if only the right doctor or the right treatment can be found, allowing it to rule his or her life. To my mind, that is paying attention to escaping from the illness. What I mean is looking most carefully at exactly what the illness is like. Where does it hurt, exactly, and when? How bad is it, exactly, and how often do I feel it? What, exactly, makes it better and what worse? Have I ever had this before, and what was happening then in my life? Does it remind me of some early childhood illness or experience? Why do I have it now, at this particular time? What does it stop me doing, and what does it allow me to do which I couldn't have done before? How does it respond to particular kinds of weather, food, drink, films, company? The list is endless, and it is indeed a lot of work paying real attention to an illness. None of these questions or their answers make any sense unless you believe that illness has some point, some meaning in a person's life. But if it does, then the questions will elicit its meaning.

This takes us back to the fundamental point. An illness isn't just a localized failure which can be handed over to a mechanic to fix, as you might hand over a car with a broken engine. The symptoms of illness aren't just aberrations. They are the consequences of the system doing its best to return to balance, and demonstrating, therefore, what would help it to get there.

> *Frozen shoulder, lung infection, whatever the complaint is, it's always the same thing; something beneficial trying to happen.*

Eliot Cowan

Well, I've had severe bronchitis, a truly awful bout of flu, tonsillitis, sciatic pain, a broken leg, and depression. I remember what each of them was like at the time, and it certainly wouldn't have been easy, or even plausible, to think of them as 'something beneficial trying to happen'. But from personal experience and from seeing what happens to my patients, I now think it is true. The 'something beneficial' may not be nice at all; it may appear to the conscious mind as, at best, an awful nuisance, or, at worst, as a bitterly unjust and cruel hardship. I wouldn't dream of making light of the pain and suffering of those with serious and debilitating illnesses. But I can see in my own illnesses, and those of the people I treat, this 'something beneficial' trying to break through like the sun on a grey and cloudy day. I can see illness as an indication, usually unwelcome, of what we need to do or what we need to be. In short, we don't always know, can't always know, what our life is about, what is our part to play. We may not be who we think we are. And when illness nudges – or forces – us towards knowing, we'll probably recoil from the prospect. As C. S. Lewis said so memorably, 'I had to be dragged, kicking and screaming, over the threshold of the kingdom of heaven.'

All this may seem terribly spiritual and hence far removed from the often mundane business of the body's problems and needs, which are especially mundane during illness. But I think it is central. The body isn't a machine. It is, as Jung puts it in the heading quote, 'the outward manifestation of the life of the spirit'. That implies that its ailments are, at root, spiritual ailments. They are indications that all is not well at a deeper level, a level whose messages come to us through all kinds of oblique language such as dreams, symptoms, chance remarks which we never forget, unexpected moments of pure happiness, bizarre difficulties in what seemed to be a simple plan, and so on. This view is expressed by many teachers and practitioners in many ways; the following is my favourite:

> *Illness exists first*
>
> *in the non-physical realm*
>
> *of spiritual need,*
>
> *emotional confusion,*
>
> *or mental aberration.*
>
> *It is never primarily physical.*
>
> *The body is the reactor.*
>
> *It vibrates to stress*
>
> *and is an outward manifestation*
>
> *of inner turmoil.*

> Emmanuel

Ask yourself if this doesn't ring true to you, if it doesn't fit the facts of illnesses you have had. He goes on:

> *As the body constricts*
>
> *under the onslaught of trauma,*
>
> *there is a denial of energy*

to a particular part of the body.

Thus the stage is set

for a physical manifestation

which is, in your reality,

a malfunction of the body.

This is a wonderfully succinct explanation of why energy medicine works. If there is a 'denial of energy to a particular part of the body', and that leads to a 'malfunction' then restoring energy to that part should help to restore proper functioning. And when energy seeps back into that part it isn't surprising that patients often remember a distressing incident, sometimes a very old one, which they'd forgotten. The 'denial of energy' has kept the memory of the trauma insulated from the rest of the mind and body, as if in a vacuum flask. Simply remembering can be a key stage in healing. Once you know what is making you suffer it is at least possible to do something about it. If you don't know, you're at a loss to know what to do for the best.

The quotation also points to the limitations of energy medicine. If the denial of energy to one part of the body is acute and long lasting, then it may be practically impossible to restore energy to that part. In the terms of Chapter 6, there isn't enough energy there to resonate with a healthy vibration introduced by colour, sound, homeopathic remedies, herbs, needles, crystals, magnets – whatever the technique. The patient will need some other form of medicine, or some other form of medicine first. And it may also be that the tissue has become so damaged through lack of energy that it can't heal. Then surgery is a sensible option. Removing the damaged tissue may allow blood, lymph, and energy to flow again through the area, and to feed other parts of the body which have been starved because of the blockage there.

As more and more people have some form of energy medicine, these ideas and these attitudes to illness will start to have a wide influence. For one thing, patients will start to take more responsibility both for their health and for their illnesses. They won't expect to remain passive, taking no genuine interest in the causes of their complaints and their route to health, and expecting someone else to fix it for them. This will affect the way they interact with their doctors and the way they use conventional medicine – sometimes even as complementary to energy medicine . For those doctors who have lived and practised in an earlier era, one where most patients had a different attitude, I can imagine that this may be very difficult. But I can also imagine that it will be a source of immense relief, even liberation, to a younger generation of doctors. It must be unbearably stressful to be put in a position where you are expected to have an answer to every problem, a cure for every illness – especially when you know you haven't. You have to struggle to help when you know you can't. And you'll be thought to have failed when there was nothing you could have done.

And as these ideas become commonplace, it isn't hard to imagine changes in everything from medical research to the design of hospitals to the organization of health care. Overwhelmingly, medical research is devoted to the causes of illness and to devising drugs to remove those causes. What about research into wellness? No one studies people who don't get flu when all around them succumb, who don't get lung cancer in spite of years of smoking, who enjoy life to the full from a wheelchair. Instead of trying to find out how it is that some untrained and unqualified healers get genuinely remarkable results, the researchers look the other way. If it is the stimulation of a person's own healing potential which is instrumental in bringing about change, then how would hospitals be designed and run to amplify that potential? And what will be the effect on a National Health Service if it is accepted that such a service should provide the kinds of medicine that people choose rather than simply the kind they are given?

I am sure that changes are afoot. They won't come from practitioners of energy medicine, nor from doctors, nor from hospital administrators, nor from politicians. They will come from patients who have had the courage to break the mould in some way: the ones who have had the willingness to investigate their own illnesses, the wisdom to trust what they discover, and the determination to get whatever help they need. These pioneers will create the health care of the future.

Appendix

Forms of energy medicine

There is no definitive list of therapies or techniques which count as forms of energy medicines. For one thing, reasonable people will disagree about the criteria for inclusion, and for another, I'm sure I don't know all the therapies which could or should be included. With that suitably cowardly caveat, here are two lists.

The first contains the therapies which I consider to be undoubtedly energy medicine and which, to a greater or lesser extent, this book seeks to explain. Essentially, I see them all as variations on one theme, as based on the same partial truth about the body and how it works.

The second list includes a number of therapies which do not claim to be forms of energy medicine, but which, in my experience, work at least in part because of the effect they have on the energy body. Much of what I have written applies to them, I think, although their practitioners may not agree.

Obviously, but I feel I have to say it, inclusion in these lists is not some kind of endorsement or recommendation of a particular therapy – still less of anyone who practises it.

List 1

Acupuncture
Aromatherapy
Aura-Soma
Ayurveda
Bowen technique
Colour therapies
Crystal healing
Flower remedies
Herbal medicine
Kinesiology
Kosmed
Light therapies
Metamorphic technique
Magnet therapies
Reflexology
Reiki
Sound healing
Shiatsu
Tui Na
Zero balancing

List 2

Alexander technique
Cranial osteopathy
Cranio-sacral therapy
Feldenkrais
Heller work
McTimoney chiropractic
Rolfing

Select bibliography

I have used all these books time and time again. Out of a huge range of books on this subject, they are the ones that have consistently illuminated the issues and taught me a lot.

Radical Healing Dr Rudolph Ballentine, Rider, London 1999
I've put this first because it is a wonderful book: comprehensive, authoritative, and very well written. It manages to explain the most esoteric ideas in a perfectly straightforward way, and never slides away from the difficulties. Almost uniquely in this area, the analysis is rigorous.

The Healing Arts – a journey through the faces of medicine Ted Kaptchuk and Michael Croucher, BBC, London 1986
The book of a TV series which was well ahead of its time. The book ranges widely, is based on real scholarship, and is always fascinating. It is eloquent and written with real passion.

Love, Medicine and Miracles Bernie S. Siegel, Arrow, London 1988
A bestseller and a classic. The author is a practising surgeon who sees his work very differently from most practitioners of Western medicine, as part of a long tradition of healing to which he adds what has been learned recently by therapists from all sorts of other disciplines and backgrounds.

Ida Rolf talks about Rolfing and Physical Reality Ida Rolf, ed.
Rosemary Feitis, Harper & Rowe, New York 1978
A series of short pieces taken from her teachings and conversation. Full of wisdom and insight into the body and how it
works – the kind of stuff that you've never thought of before
but as soon as you read it you say, 'Oh. Of course.' And full of
a sharp, wisecracking American humour.

Anatomy of an Illness Norman Cousins, W. W. Norton,
New York & London 1979
A personal account of a serious illness, which widens out into
reflections on conventional treatments, their validity, and
the path he took instead – back to health. A pioneer as a
person and a pioneering book.

Inner Bridges, A guide to energy movement and body structure
Fritz Frederick Smith, Humanics, Atlanta, Georgia, 1986
This is a remarkable integration of a deep knowledge of
Western anatomy and physiology with a deep experience of
the way energy flows in the human body, so that, unusually,
they complement each other.

The Man who Mistook his Wife for a Hat Oliver Sacks,
Picador, London, 1985
Another classic and deserved bestseller. A set of gripping
stories in which the best in people shines through the most
bizarre and difficult illnesses. And the best in what it means
to be a doctor shines through too.

Plant Spirit Medicine Eliot Cowan, Swan Raven, Oregon 1995
This book contains the best description I know of the five
elements (referred to in Chapter 2 of this book). It also
provides a lucid and convincing explanation of the most
apparently magical healing powers of plants.

Genome: the autobiography of a species in 23 chapters
Matt Ridley, Fourth Estate, London, 2000
An outstanding example of what is called popular science. It
is moving, witty, and explains more about human biology
than a thousand textbooks.

Energy Medicine: the scientific basis James L. Oschman,
Churchill Livingstone, London 2000
A clear summary of a host of scientific research and a sober
assessment of developments which might lead to new forms
of treatment, as well as providing validation for some very
ancient ones.

Infinite Mind, Science of the Human Vibrations of Consciousness
Valerie V. Hunt, Malibu Publishing Co, Malibu, CA 1989
An easier read than it sounds. This book goes from solid
research science to spiritual enlightenment in one leap,
without leaving the reader behind. The author is a great
scientist and a remarkable person who hasn't yet received
the widespread acclaim she deserves.

The Science of Homeopathy George Vithoulkas, Thorsons,
London 1980
Although this is a basic textbook, it is much more than that.
Wide-ranging, it explains how energy works in the body, and
puts forward an overall view of how and why people fall ill
and get better.

What really works – the insider's guide to natural health
Susan Clark, Thorsons, London 2000
By far the best compendium of complementary therapies.
Clear, convincing, and sensibly comprehensive (in that it
excludes what would be a waste of time and effort).

Notes

Overview: A time of change

The story of the acupuncture treatment comes from Fritz Frederick Smith, *Inner Bridges – a guide to energy movement and body structure*, Humanics, Atlanta, Georgia, 1986, pp. 182-3.

Chapter 1

The heading quote is from *Ida Rolf talks about Rolfing and Physical Reality*, ed. Rosemary Feitis, Harper & Rowe, New York, 1978, pp. 33-4.

The S.T. Coleridge quote is from *Coleridge, Aids to Reflection*, Routledge, London, 1993, pp. 397-8.

The asthma quote is from Dr Rudolph Ballentine, *Radical Healing*, Rider, London, 1999, pp. 85-6.

The Shakespeare sonnet is number 73.

The man with the tumour comes from Paul Pearsall, *The Heart's Code*, Broadway Books, New York, 1998, pp. 1-2.

The quote about psychosomatic illness comes from Bernie S. Siegel, *Love, Medicine and Miracles*, HarperPerennial, New York, 1990 p. 111.

The experiment with two people sitting together is described in Valerie V. Hunt, *Infinite Mind*, Malibu Publishing Co., Malibu, CA, 1989, pp. 28-9.

The quote about electromedical researchers is from Valerie V. Hunt, op. cit., p. 244.

Chapter 2

The heading quote is from Norman Cousins, *Anatomy of an Illness*, W.W. Norton, New York & London, 1979, pp. 72-3.

The piece about germs not being the sole cause of disease comes from Dr Rudolph Ballentine, op. cit., p. 142.

The quote about the genome comes from Matt Ridley, *Genome; The autobiography of a species in 23 chapters*, Fourth Estate, London, 2000, pp. 148 and 153-4.

The surgeon who watches miracles daily is Bernie S. Siegel in *Peace, Love and Healing*, Arrow, London, 1988, p. 44.

The quote about the nature of healing is from Stephen Levine, *Healing into Life and Death*, Gateway Books, Bath, 1989, p. 4.

The Llama of Crystal Mountain comes from Peter Matthieson, *The Snow Leopard*, Harvill Press, London, 1978, p. 225.

Chapter 3

The heading quote is from Robert O. Becker and Gary Selden, *The Body Electric*, Quill, William Morrow, New York, 1985, p. 47.

The quote on how energy flows down the spine comes from Fritz Frederick Smith, op. cit., p. 49.

The quote about meridians in the embryo is from Richard Gerber, *Vibrational Medicine*, Bear and Company, Santa Fe, 1988, p. 126.

The journalist's story is by Susan Clark, *The Times* (3), London, 28th September 1999, p. 38.

The insight that depression is accompanied by chronically shortened flexor muscles is from Moshe Feldenkrais, *Awareness Through Movement – health exercises for personal growth*, Arkana, London, 1990.

Chapter 4

The heading quote is from Caroline Myss and C. Norman Shealy, *The Creation of Health*, Bantam Books, London, 1999, pp. 61-2. It is virtually a quotation from a 19th and early 20th century physician, Sir William Osler, quoted in Peter Adams, *The Soul of Medicine*, Penguin, London, 1999, p. 67.

Carol Rayman's story is by Barbara Lentell and comes from *The Daily Telegraph*, 19th July 1999, p. 14.

Watching the posture of a child comes from Ida Rolf, op. cit., pp. 191 and 193.

The quotation 'an elderly Chinese doctor with whom I once studied' comes from Ted J. Kaptchuk, *Chinese Medicine; the web that has no weaver*, Rider, London, 1983, p. 251.

The quote about diagnosis by intuition is from Caroline Myss and C. Norman Shealy, op. cit., p. 98.

The story of Yeshi Dhonden is from Ram Dass and Paul Gorman, *How can I help?* Rider, London, 1986, p. 119.

Chapter 5

The heading quote is from Norman Cousins, op. cit., pp. 68-9.

The X-rays of spines comes from Andrew Weil, *Spontaneous Healing*, Alfred A. Knopf, New York, 1995, p. 120.

The quote about a guy whose back or hip is out comes from Ida Rolf, op. cit., p. 171.

The case of Dr P. is in Oliver Sacks, *The Man who Mistook his Wife for a Hat*, Touchstone, New York, 1970, pp. 11-12 and 18.

The quote about positive emotions is from Norman Cousins op. cit., pp. 34-5.

The quote about being well is from John Hamwee, *Zero Balancing; touching the energy of bone*, Frances Lincoln, London, 1999, p. 98.

The Jung quote I found in Liz Greene, *The Astrology of Fate*, HarperCollins, London, 1985, p. 314. I don't know the original source.

Chapter 6

The heading quote is by Ted Kaptchuk, op.cit., p. 259.

The quotation about vibrations comes from a series of articles by James L. Oschman in the *Journal of Bodywork and Movement Therapies*, July 1997, p. 240.

Technically, there is a distinction between resonance and entrainment, and strictly some of my examples are of entrainment. But the two concepts are very similar, and for the sake of simplicity, I have chosen to ignore the distinction.

The quote about heart cells is in Paul Pearsall, op. cit., p. 63.

Experiments carried out on practitioners who claimed to be able to heal simply by touch are reported in James L. Oschman, *Energy medicine; the scientific basis*, Churchill Livingstone, London 2000, pp. 78-9. The experiments with people in a sealed room come from the same book, p. 101.

The quotation about colour comes from Brian Keenan, *An Evil Cradling*, an account of time he spent in captivity, quoted in Philippa Merivale, *Healing with Colour*, Element Books, Shaftesbury, 1998, p. 3.

The quotation about the chakras comes from Barbara Ann Brennan, *Hands of Light – a guide to healing through the human energy field*, Bantam Books, New York, 1988, p. 241.

The Bernie S. Siegel quote is from *Peace, Love and Healing*, p. 6.

The Jung quote comes from C. G. Jung, *Modern Man in Search of a Soul*, Routledge, London, 1984, p. 271.

The examples of usnea and holly essence, and the quotation about resonance, come from Dr Rudolph Ballentine, op. cit., p. 28.

I leaned the concept of a clearer, stronger, force field from Fritz Frederick Smith MD.

I realize that some of the therapies mentioned at the start of the section called 'Touch' may not regard themselves as energy medicine – Rolfing, for example. Certainly some of these therapies change and manipulate body structure; and in some cases this is their primary purpose. I've included them here because they all have a direct and powerful effect on the energy body and at least some of their practitioners work deliberately and explicitly with it. Ida Rolf, who certainly manipulated structure, was well aware that she was working with energy too – see *Remembering Ida Rolf*, ed. Rosemary Feitis and Louis Schultz, North Atlantic Books, Berkley CA, 1996, pp. 56 and 223.

The medical techniques quote is from Robert O. Becker and Gary Selden, op. cit., p. 18.

Chapter 7

The heading quote is from Ted Kaptchuk and Michael Croucher, *The Healing Arts – a journey through the faces of medicine*, BBC, London, 1986, p. 152.

The powerful woman lawer comes from Rachel Naomi Remen, 'The Search for Healing' in *Healers on Healing*, ed. Carson and Shield, Jeremy P. Tarcher, Los Angeles, 1989, p93.

The story of the man with hay fever is from Eliot Cowan, *Plant Spirit Medicine*, Swan Raven, Oregon, 1995, p. 57.

The quote about states of consciousness is from William James, *Varieties of Religious Experience*, Fontana, London, 1974, p. 374.

The woman at the table is in Carol Shields, *Dressing up for the Carnival*, Vintage Canada, Toronto, 2001, p. 106.

'Much light, much peace' comes from Ram Dass, *Still Here: embracing ageing, changing, and dying*, Riverhead Books, New York, 2000, p. 73.

Conclusion: Patients

The heading quote is from C. G. Jung, op. cit., pp. 253-4.

The quotation about frozen shoulder is from Eliot Cowan, op. cit., pp. 39-40.

I haven't been able to find the source of the quote attributed to C. S. Lewis.

The quotation about the nature of illness is from *Emmanuel's Book*, compiled by Pat Rodegast and Judith Stanton, Bantam Books, New York, 1987, p 159.

Index